The Spiritual CEO

S. Prakash, the CEO of See Change, India, is a nationally acclaimed author, coach, master storyteller, keynote speaker, heartful leader, organisational turnaround expert and nation builder. His three-and-a-half decades of work includes a rich blend of business, management and leadership experiences. He has been writing on human behaviour, business success and other related topics for over two decades. He has published ten books in several languages and has authored more than a thousand articles on self-development, spirituality and other subjects.

The Spiritual CEO is based on his understanding of Indian mythology, corporate lifecycles and its connection to leadership and organisational shifts globally. An avid reader, he has been practising Heartfulness Meditation since 1992, and is a certified Heartfulness trainer. Thanks to his corporate life and the Heartfulness Institute, he has worked with people from across the world.

He is secretary to Daaji, the global guide and president of Heartfulness Institute.

AF875119

Praise for the Book

Leadership is a fascinating subject for me. This book draws from mythology and brings fresh perspectives through storytelling. It offers a new approach for leaders to self-reflect. I happily recommend this book to all.

– Vani Kola, managing director, Kalaari Capital

'What gets passed down from your predecessor in this pivotal role of CEO, is not just about financials, products, customers, etc. alone. You will be inheriting a huge balance of Korporate Karma that is set to play a crucial role in steering the course of the ship during your tenure.' This opener to the last chapters—'The Metamorphosis of a CEO' and 'The New Terra Firma'—is superbly written. In my view, this book is the first-ever 'management thriller' with balanced views to cover all facets of leadership and the role of a CEO for the emerging 'new normal'. I would strongly urge every corporate leader to have a copy of this book for bedside reading.

– Sanjay Bhatia, IAS, chairman, Mumbai Port Trust
(In the rank of secretary, GOI)

As the world moves on from IQ to EQ to SQ, business guru S. Prakash hits the bullseye with an exposition on the 'spiritual' CEO behind the SQ (spiritual quotient). It is an essential reading for all aspirants to lead and transform their organisations and prepare for the challenges ahead. This book has come at the right time as the world grapples with a pandemic that threatens to disrupt the physical, mental and spiritual equilibrium of individuals, societies and nations.

– Rishabh C. Kothari, CEO, CKC Fragrances, president,
Fragrances & Flavours Association of India [FAFAI] and vice president,
Merchants Chamber of Commerce & Industry [MCCI]

The Spiritual CEO by S. Prakash links the essence of pauranik and ethical values in corporate administration. It's a novel and noble thought. This landmark work is bound to make a valuable contribution to corporate businesses practices on ethical lines. A must-have in every corporate library.

– A. L. Somayaji, senior advocate, Chennai and
former advocate general of Tamil Nadu

A very well written book. Crisp and clear. Easy to understand. Lots of depth in the examples given and also in the book overall. A must-read for all CEOs irrespective of the size of their organisation. In fact, world leaders and people of every walk of life can and must use this book as a reference guide to help them be more successful and inspiring leaders.

I can feel and see his many years of experience in training and guiding the corporate world in how the content has been approached and written. Kudos! It is a privilege that I could read the book and share my thoughts.

– Kris Srinaath, former cricketer

The role of a CEO and leader has been undergoing a significant transformation over the last few decades, mostly driven by increased globalisation, digitisation and pace of innovation. Many of the fundamentals that a CEO needs to deliver—such as returning profits to the company's investors—continue to remain relevant. However, to be 'successful' in the eyes of employees, shareholders and other stakeholders—a CEO needs to look beyond 'just financials' into different dimensions of corporate well-being. Over the last two decades, we have seen increased scrutiny of a company's performance in 'intangible' measurements such as social responsibility, corporate values, employee well-being and related facets. This book brings out terrific perspectives that would help the reader hone his skills at the topmost level and become a true *sthitpragya* or a balanced CEO. I heartily recommend this book to every CEO and aspiring CEO, as well.

– V.K. Jhaver, chairman and MD, Tropical Agrosystem (I) Pvt. Ltd., India.

S. Prakash has been exploring spirituality, philosophy, corporate governance and life in general for many years. He takes a fresh look at things.

In this book, he puts across a convincing set of logical arguments to drive home the apparent set of paradoxical concepts of spiritual values to CEOs, who are essentially responsible for making profits and increasing shareholder value in the shortest possible tenure. Set in the Indian context, he draws generously from the ancient scriptures and mythology. He has a conversational style with a blend of humour to make the reading light while retaining the seriousness that the topics deserve.

This is a brilliant work by Prakash and a must-read for CEOs, VPs, directors, to-be-CEOs and boardroom executives. A proper understanding of this book will usher in a paradigm shift in the governing values of the corporate culture. The value lies in the lasting culture of a corporation in making a difference to humanity.

– Victor Kannan, Career CFO, USA and lifelong volunteer for Heartfulness, USA.

Prakash has written a must-read spiritual management book. It is one of its kind for those considering integrating spirituality into their business. Every CEO and potential CEO must read this book ... and learn from one of the best. I have started implementing it myself.

– Dr Rajmohan Pillai, bestselling author; chairman, Beta Group

I read through the book. It's wonderfully written with a captivating style of writing! In today's world of uncertainties, this could be a useful roadmap for every leader (not just CEOs) to lead their businesses, communities, families and lives. A must-read for all leaders and CEOs.

– Sanjay Sehgal, chairman and CEO of MSys Group, USA and compulsive entrepreneur, global businessman, startup advisor, keynote speaker, philanthropist, mindful and Heartful human

This is a fantastic book, written simply and lucidly by S. Prakash. The question-answer format makes the otherwise difficult spiritual concepts easy to understand. *The Spiritual CEO* is a must-read for all CEOs, aspiring-CEOs, and leaders across hierarchies. It will shed new light on the way you see your work.

– Sameer Dua, social activist, bestselling author and founder-director, The Institute for Generative Leadership

The Spiritual CEO serves as a guide and reinforcement of the 'spiritual ethics', as one leads a corporate organisation or as a leader in general. Quoting extensively from mythology, and written in a simple, lucid style, the author highlights the applications of these spiritual principles in modern-day life and leaves you with key takeaways. The book underlines the importance of weaving spirituality into the corporate and material life, to facilitate a 'balanced living' in current times.

– Dr. Pramod Sadarjoshi, founder and CEO, Talentsmith Consulting

The Spiritual CEO by S. Prakash, carefully links the past and present with key takeaways and action plans for the better future of CEOs and their business. It is a ready reckoner for the success of CEOs. It's a must-read for entrepreneurs and would-be-entrepreneurs.

– M. Jagadeesh, advocate and peacemaker, Bangalore

Prakash provides an interesting, intriguing and uncommon set of perspectives for business leaders, in this book. It is an accessible read with stories from mythology generously used to draw perspectives. The views he shares are best verified by attempting some of his suggestions at the end of each chapter and testing their effect on the organisation.

– Prashanth Vasu, partner, McKinsey & Company, Inc.

The world is moving from IQ to EQ to SQ to AQ. A CEO is the chief of versatility and ethical standards of an organisation and its overall environment. The book, *The Spiritual CEO* mentions examples of Bhakta Prahlad, Abhimanyu and Kautilya for developing and balancing Korporate Karma. As the custodian of an organisation, a CEO must maintain a balance between body, mind and soul for the organisational effectiveness. This is possible only through in-depth knowledge of the cause and the ability to exit from the Chakravyuha. A spiritual CEO combines ethical standards with performance skills and knowledge which may well be understood by reading the book. I recommend that every CEO and CEO-in-the-making must read and practice the learnings in *The Spiritual CEO*.

– Brij Mohan Prasad, training and management consultant, fellow ISTD and fellow NIPM and advocate, Jharkhand High Court, Ranchi.

The corporate world and the spiritual realm are mutually exclusive, is an idea that most of us have been asked to profess. Though we may have known that the belief is flawed, we haven't thought of busting the myth. *The Spiritual CEO* is an excellent source to reaffirm our thoughts that a CEO could imbibe a plethora of aphorisms from the spiritual arena to give his role more meaning and stability. The author has phrased the book lucidly to make it an enjoyable read!

– Sri Dushyanth Sridhar, Indic speaker and writer, www.desikadaya.org

The Spiritual CEO is not just another book on the bookshelf, it is a companion for the journey. This book is not just for CEOs; it's for every individual who is starting their journey into corporate life, entrepreneurship, leading teams (big and small) and engaging and dealing with fellow human beings. S Prakash sets the tone of the journey as being important in everything we do as a 'lead indicator' versus just the outcome being 'lag indicator' by using the Cause and Effect theory. This needs to be imbibed by one and all, right from early walks of life, so that it becomes a habit to do things the right way, eventually getting results.

– Suryanarayanan B, VP, sales and BD (APAC), Privafy Inc

The Spiritual CEO is an amazing guide that highlights the role of Spiritual Quotient in the transformation of a CEO during these times of VUCA (Volatility, Uncertainty, Complexity, and Ambiguity). This book is a road map for both CEOs and all 'Thought Leaders' to imbibe corporate values and ethics in an organisation's DNA. The author vividly blends learning from our roots, Indian culture and mythology and explains how to start this experiential journey through spirituality.

– Nupur Ray, Happiness coach, head, employee engagement, Bajaj Allianz Life Insurance Co. Ltd.

The Spiritual CEO by S. Prakash is a fantastic book. I sincerely feel that it must be read by every professional. In today's complex world, books like this are reference points for professionals like me to get clarity on problems and guidance on how to troubleshoot them.

Simplicity is another interesting aspect of this book.

– Shirish R Kamble (PMP, CSM), project leader, Western Union Technology and Engineering Center, Pune.

An exceptionally well-written book. By definition, a spiritual person practices Dharmic values like exemplary moral and ethical standards, practicing and defending truth, and above all unconditional compassion for people, as prescribed in ancient epics like Mahabharata.

Prakash beautifully connects to that value system and highlights the importance of spiritual practices in making a leader a 'Total Leader'.He points out that it is insufficient to have technical and business skills alone to become an exemplary leader. One must also have the characteristic of a truly spiritual person who thinks for others. This is where the SQ comes into play. In this world where it is rare to find an egoless leader, Mr Prakash's book is a reminder to such people that there is little chance for them to reach the 'mountain of choice' without sincere application of Spiritual IQ.

In addition to being a great companion for current CEOs, this book could be a textbook for MBA students aspiring to become future leaders. Mr Prakash's lucid style of writing makes it easy to read, understand and comprehend. I heartily recommend this book.

– K.S. Radhakrishnan, member of the board, DISYS Corporation, USA; Retd. VP, global IT operations, Boeing

The Spiritual CEO covers aspects of management that are consistently overlooked. It offers insights into using the right intention, ethics-based thinking and one's own heart's compass to build better teams and organisations. It inspired me to think deeper. The 'Action Points' section, at the end of each chapter, offers insight on how to take these aspects from the realm of philosophy and put them to practice.

– Punit Lalbhai, executive director, Arvind Ltd.

S.PRAKASH

THE SPIRITUAL CEO

First published by Westland Publications Private Limited in 2021

1st Floor, A Block, East Wing, Plot No. 40, SP Infocity, Dr MGR Salai, Perungudi, Kandanchavadi, Chennai 600096

Westland and the Westland logo are the trademarks of Westland Publications Private Limited, or its affiliates.

Copyright © S. Prakash, 2021

ISBN: 9789390679171

10 9 8 7 6 5 4 3 2 1

The views and opinions expressed in this work are the author's own and the facts are as reported by him, and the publisher is in no way liable for the same.

All rights reserved

Typeset by Jojy Philip, New Delhi - 110015
Printed at Thomson Press (India) Ltd.

No part of this book may be reproduced, or stored in a retrieval system, or transmitted in any form or by any means, electronic, mechanical, photocopying, recording, or otherwise, without express written permission of the publisher.

MIX
Paper
FSC FSC® C010615

To my beloved Daaji, global guide, Heartfulness Institute;
my life partner Sandhya and my daughter Sukanya;
and my teachers, coaches, business friends and acquaintances,
from whom I have learnt a lot.

Contents

Foreword

My Guru Babuji Maharaj once said, 'A good heart, benevolent feelings and a balanced mind lies at the foundation of character.' Once a person's heart is in the right place, all other leadership aspects fall into place in a balanced manner. The CEO of a company functions as the heart of the organisation. To be successful, a CEO has to balance many functions. Hence, it is important for them to learn how to attain balance in both their inner condition and the many external factors around them.

'CEO' is such a generic term, yet it signifies an important position in an organisation. The CEO of a philanthropic institution is different from the CEO of a gambling company. Yet, both perform many of the same tasks. The secret of their success, no matter what business they are working in, is the intention with which their tasks are performed. It is imperative to ask, are they implemented with a heartfelt intention? A CEO builds an organisation, whereas a spiritual CEO builds a society, the benefits of which are felt by generations to come.

Expanding consciousness is an essential element in the life of a spiritual CEO. The journey towards the innermost being, the soul, is an important one if they want to understand their own capability and align with others around them. Yoga has become well recognised over the years as a means to achieve this inner and outer alignment, as it brings union with the highest Self and ensures inner stability. The result is a sense of contentment, stability and balance.

This book, written by S. Prakash, explores the journey undertaken by one such CEO to become a spiritual CEO. Each step is narrated, with examples, and it will help others who wish to travel a similar path. The connection between having a good heart and the expansion of consciousness becomes evident here. A good heart functions without feeling pressure or tension and does not negatively influence the mind with desires, fears, ego, ignorance and prejudice. A person without these negative influences does not attract karma, so we can say that a spiritual CEO is one who acts without building negative 'Korporate Karma'. The simple art of meditation with the support of yogic Transmission can do wonders to build such a carefree open heart. When the CEO, the heart of an organisation, is experiencing and radiating positivity and charging the environment with joy, a positive working atmosphere ensues.

Expanding consciousness (*chit*) involves refining the senses, the mind (*manas*), the intellect (*buddhi*) and the ego (*ahankara*). As a result, the corporate CEO evolves from being a self-focussed individual to a person with a broader collective vision. Every decision of a spiritual CEO is taken for all within his or her sphere of impact. And an expanded consciousness is vital for fulfilling this responsibility. In fact, the decision-making process depends heavily on having a higher perspective. Spiritual CEOs strive to maintain equanimity through both success and failure, a state explained in the Bhagavad Gita as *sthitpragya*. S. Prakash has touched upon these levels in every chapter with appropriate stories from our ancient texts, drawing parallels with current scenarios prevailing in the corporate world.

This book is a step-by-step evolution of the CEO Journey, so it has a special place amidst the current uncertainty and transformation we see in the corporate sector. Organisations are aware today that they need to focus on integrity and ethics. So they promote their values openly to encourage alignment from management, employees, customers and partners alike. For an organisation to imbibe spiritual values, the CEO must be spiritually elevated and should practise those values. The inner and outer states of the CEO must conjoin. The motivation for profit is fine as long as it is backed by honesty and sincerity, bringing value to society. This alignment is possible only when the CEO has a good heart and a balanced mind. This requires effort and does not happen by accident. In the current digital age, this concept can become a *Mahavakya,* as described in the scriptures. The Mandukya Upanishad says that the more a person reflects on the truth, the more it reveals itself and displays that person's connections with the truth.

This book examines the effect of a CEO's actions on the DNA of an organisation. It also highlights the journey from rudimentary management to becoming genuinely concerned about society at large. When any society recognises the value of an organisation, growth is assured on all fronts. A spiritual CEO bridges the society and the organisation through this good-hearted approach. This aspiration is a step in the right direction towards bringing our traditional values into the modern corporate culture.

Daaji, Global Guide of Heartfulness Meditation

Preface

If I had come across an unusually titled book like *The Spiritual CEO*, a decade ago, I would have wondered if I should even read it. Why would CEOs opt for a book with a title that sounds like an oxymoron then, when they have so many reading options available? If you find yourself thinking along these lines, you are not alone.

However, the scenario today, as it stands in the first half of 2021 CE, presents a different picture.

Globally, the pandemic has impacted organisations and the way they function, and this changed scenario calls for an entirely new set of integrated ideologies and a different approach.

It is no longer sufficient to evaluate a CEO's performance based on a phenomenal increase in profits, turnover or other financial aspects alone. The need for a broader outlook is being discussed across corporate boardrooms, albeit in undertones. And there is more to these conversations than integrity or ethics. Thes discussions are gaining momentum to reach out to the critical mass and create ripples across the cross-section of corporate structures.

The new corporate mantra emerging from boardroom discussions I have been privy to is 'Korporate Karma'. What gets passed down from predecessors in this pivotal role of the CEO is not just information about financials, products, customers, etc.

CEOs will be inheriting a huge balance of *Korporate Karma* that is set to play a crucial role in steering the business during your tenure.

Let us look into the fundamental aspects of Korporate Karma and the power it wields over the destiny of every organisation. At the outset, it is evident that these aspects may not resonate with your belief system or of the Indian mystical and metaphysical concepts linked to one's life and destiny. Instead, it should be linked to a value chain mapping, beginning-to-end, of a 'Cause-Effect' model. It is a matrix with an immense impact on your organisation, its performance, and its future than can be conceived. Living in denial of its influences is no longer a choice.

With the COVID-19 pandemic striking at the roots of the world's social and economic infrastructure, the CEOs of this century will be faced with a whole set of new challenges, for which they need to be prepared, sooner or later. This is a rude wake-up call. The messages that are there now for everyone to read can no longer be ignored or brushed aside as some random happenings of a transient nature. The repercussions and the impact on the future of the world looms large over every individual.

We are in an intricately connected world, and so is the cause-effect conundrum of all those who are in your chain of Web-weave of internal and external connections. It takes time to understand the complex nature of the butterfly effect, but today it is commonly quoted in all walks of life. *The same will happen to the term Korporate Karma in light of the Cause-Effect application, where it will soon become the 'new normal'*.

The book is an easy read and has questions raised by several board members and 'C' suite leaders from different backgrounds and verticals. It covers riveting topics of great importance to you, as the CEO, and is kept in a conversational style (like a Q&A session). All topics you pick up and deep dive into will provide you with insights into a different dimension. In all these conversations, we are still not moving away from the old-fashioned requirement of a CEO—WIFM or WIFMO (what is in it for me or what is in it for my organisation). The performance or financial success of the organisation has not been sidelined in these conversations. After all, CEOs are still answerable to the board, the investors et al, right?

I recommend that you read the book cover to cover for a comprehensive view if you can. But if you are looking for guidance in a specific area—you can jump directly to the particular chapter. Go on. Use this book as a learning kit, a ready reckoner, a conscience prompter or whatever you choose to name it.

You know you have made the right choice in picking up this book as it will provide you with an additional set of new paradigms and perceptions you might not have been able to pick up from any other CEO book. The world is going through a tremendous transformation—a palpable metamorphosis—and we, as leaders, have the ability and expertise to manage the challenges compassionately. How can it be made possible? Inculcating spiritual values into our corporate culture and its working is the only solution. The change will have to begin with us as leaders, and the kind of practices and mechanisms we set up for this purpose ought to trickle down to every employee in the organisation.

Gender-specific terms have been used to ease the flow of the content and conversations throughout the book. Readers are requested to understand it as a reference to both genders unless explicitly stated.

1

What is Your Korporate Karma?

As I walked into the office of Corporate Yogi, I saw him absorbed in a book. I knew instantly. It was the Mahabharata, the magnum opus of our times. He had often told me about how he had developed a passion for the epic, right from his childhood days, and how he found it to be a source of perennial knowledge. According to him, the process of acquiring true knowledge involves learning, unlearning and relearning.

He looked up and greeted me with his characteristic warmth and smile. I knew he was working on another one of his books, and eager to know how it was shaping up, I brought up the topic in our conversation. He said he had just finished writing about an incident from the Mahabharata as an introductory story to the first chapter, 'What Is Korporate Karma?'

'Korporate Karma?' Enjoying my puzzled expression, he went about reading the epic story in his own inimitable style. It began with a relevant verse from a chapter of the Shrimad Bhagavad Gita. He planned to use one for each chapter, throughout the book.

avinashi tu tadviddhi yena sarvamidam tatam
vinasham avyayasyasya na kashchit kartum arhati | |

That which pervades the entire world, cannot be destroyed. No one can cause the destruction of that which does not change.

|| Gita Ch.2-V.17 ||

The Curse on Lord Krishna—A Lesson on Karma

The Mahabharat war was at last over. Was there really a purpose behind the gory dance of death and destruction? Gandhari had lost all her magnificent sons. The inconsolable mother spat out a venomous curse at Lord Krishna: '*May the same fate befall you and your entire tribe!*' A curtain-raiser to the finale of the drama of seething vendetta! Krishna had foreseen the end and had prayed and got a son like Shiva, the God of Destruction. This son, Samba, was to spearhead the destruction of His clan.

Intoxicated by their abundant prosperity, the Yadavas played a prank on the sages Vishwamitra and Durvasa when they visited Dwaraka. Samba dressed up like a pregnant lady, and the great sages were asked to predict the sex of the child. The boy received their wrath and delivered an iron mace (which was to cause the destruction of the Yadava clan). The Yadavas powdered and cast the mace into the river, which grew as the grass on its banks and became the weapons of destruction of the Yadavas much later. It so happened that a drunken brawl saw the Yadavas exterminating their own tribe using this grass.

Krishna decided to leave His mortal body. He applied payasam all over His body, and when He could not reach His feet, where His life was to end, He went into Yoga Samadhi under a tree. A hunter mistaking Krishna's foot for an animal shot a lethal arrow at it but realising the mistake, he bowed before the Lord.

It was a settlement of the karmic account; Krishna was born as Rama in the previous birth and had killed Vaali while hiding behind a tree. Vaali was reborn as Jara, the hunter, and the karmic account was balanced.

Krishna's exit from the world signalled the beginning of Kaliyuga.

The above narrative from Mahabharata illustrates the power of curse, the power of karma and how even the Lord himself is bound by karma (though created by his Yadava-clan to some extent). The same set of theories applies to the CEO of an organisation as well.

The message conveyed through the above short narrative set me on the path of exploring the connection between the theory of karma and a CEO. 'Can I address you in a casual manner, as Yogi'? He replied in the affirmative and readied himself to face my queries.

How does this connect to the corporate world? Is the concept of karma just for discussion in a spiritual-religious context or does it have relevance in fast-paced corporates as well?

CY: Let us look at it this way: the world is connected by an invisible network of actions and responses and everyone's path in life is constantly intersecting that of others. A logical mind easily understands the metaphor popularly known as the 'Butterfly Effect', which states that a very small change in initial conditions can create a significantly different outcome at a later stage. The concept of karma is a little more abstract and mysterious for the human mind to grasp. Its impact on the movement of life on earth has come to be accepted as beyond the comprehensive abilities of the human mind. In the corporate world, one only has to look at the history of companies that went bankrupt in the last few decades; questionable, dubious deeds by those at the helm of affairs resulted in the collapse of those companies which were riding at the top—a direct example of karma wielding its influence.

What tangible difference will it make, in the larger realm of things, if I start believing in karma?

CY: My Guru used to say, 'What the brain doesn't know, the mind will find it difficult to comprehend'. Man's ability to interpret the ebbs and flows of life through his logical skills and knowledgeable background is extremely limited, though it is difficult for him to accept this. To understand the core concept of karma, a different perspective—a paradigm shift—is needed. The future of an individual is determined by his actions in the past and the present. A corporate is nothing but a collection of individuals and its activities fall within the purview of the same principle. To put it in the form of a common adage, 'You reap what you sow'.

A paradigm shift? What would that be?

CY: Switch over to the heart. The mind thinks, whereas the Heart experiences. With or without our knowledge and acceptance, it is through the heart that all our learning happens. This is better explained through the concept of *Samskara*, a Sanskrit word, where the prefix 'sam' means 'well-planned and well-thought-out', and 'kara' means 'action undertaken'. All our actions are preceded by thought and it is the thought that manifests into action. So, 'samskara' means 'the impression created by the impact of an action performed, while fully aware of its implications'. Whenever an action is performed consciously, a subtle impression gets deposited in the heart. Each time the same type of manifestation-of-thought-into-action sequence is repeated, the impression becomes stronger.

Now this becomes a cyclic process—actions lead to the formation of habits and habits in turn lead to actions of the same nature. People are invariably slaves of their habits, and the stronger the habits are, the more difficult it is for them to execute an action that is contrary to their habit patterns. So, we are all motivated in a subtle, yet powerful, manner, by our habit patterns. When we allow our lives to be driven by habits, we lose our ability to discriminate between what we tend to do out of habit and what actually needs to be done.

Samskaras do not differentiate between good and bad—any habitual action backed by a powerful thought creates a samskara. A warehouse of samskaras, with both positive and negative overtones, gets created in each human being. It is up to each of us to exercise our willpower and determination to strengthen or eliminate a particular group of samskaras.

Every thought and action, in the transactional and functional world, is like sowing a seed. If the seed is good and well-nourished, it bears good fruits, otherwise, there is every chance for it to wither away or become a poisonous weed. In both cases, we have the exclusive liberty to make a choice. The same holds true for the corporate world. Every day when executives, leaders and managers have to make crucial decisions—they do take inputs from the available data—but in the end, when they settle down on a list of good choices (or, for that matter, a list of not-so-great choices), the dictates of the heart get implemented—even though it may not be explicitly stated as such.

So, it implies that we can choose an effect by deciding the cause?
CY: Almost always, *yes*. We have to also concede that it cannot be applied in toto, because there could be many factors outside our sphere of control which may have to be taken into consideration before deciding on the final outcome; but within the confines of our prerogative to choose, the cause definitely plays the dominant role.

What is it that this epic story and your subsequent explanation try to convey?
CY: The quintessence of what I am trying to convey is a principle of ethics; 'Be mindful of what you sow, through your thoughts, deeds and actions'. This should be followed not only by you as an individual, but across your organisation's workforce. If you happen to be at the topmost level in an organisation, the onus is on you to see to it that every one of your employees gets trained to follow this principle. An organisation's future is continuously being written and rewritten. Imagine getting out of a swimming pool and before you dive in again, the contours have been redrawn and the water is muddy. If you jump in again at the same place assuming things will be the same, you might get injured.

To draw a comparison with day-to-day corporate life, it might be easy to set goals but the actual work is in the efforts to reach there. lag indicators (as goals or objectives are called) are of no consequence if the lead indicators (efforts or inputs that would guide you towards the goal) are not in place. Korporate Karma says that lag indicators are your 'effects' whereas the lead indicators are your 'causes'. While the former is important, Korporate Karma says focus on the lead indicators. Rather than the 'what' it is the 'how' and 'why' that matter more.

So, Korporate Karma is an arsenal in the hands of a CEO?
CY: Yes. Not only the CEO of an organisation but anyone who is in charge of dealing with people. It creates a ripple effect, after all. The CEO is not the only one who is throwing a stone in the pond! Imagine a multiple ripple effect getting created and no one is focussing on the why and how of it, with the result that utter chaos, from beginning to end, will prevail. I am not discounting the knowledge and all other resources that are essential in moving towards the goal, but there is an element that gives a twist to the tale, which CEOs have been missing for long.

Can you please elaborate?
CY: As I am talking to you, the entire world is going through an unprecedented crisis of enormous magnitude; now, did any CEO think through a backup plan for such a situation? My intention is not to blame anyone for not being able to foresee such disastrous situations, but to make people understand that there are certain things that continuously keep altering the trajectory of one's flight.

While I could look at it from multiple angles, suffice it to say that an action or an input that I didn't cause and was not directly participating in, can impact my business; in this case, big time. Any type of business with unplanned inputs from its team of employees will have to eventually face the unpleasant consequences, sometime or the other. The samskaras/scripts that my fellow colleagues and I carry on between us can cause a direct impact on the trajectory of my organisation. While I am on that trajectory and working towards ensuring things are okay as we move along, there could be meteor showers on the path (like the current Covid-19 pandemic crisis); there could be an unknown or unseen pattern that throws such curveballs in my path. Other than such catastrophes hitting like meteorites, there could be smaller pebbles that get thrown at me from the karmic labs of my competitor, my customers, vendors, et al. When it comes to such external influences, I can only have as much control as a rocket has on its computer-fed program.

Experience has repeatedly taught us humans that our lives are interwoven by connecting threads of dependence and that I cannot manage things with my intellect alone in this quagmire of unknown dimensions.

So, what should one do?
CY: To sum up this topic, let me share a simple framework. Be aware and alter—Accept and Adapt.

Would you mind expanding a bit on this, please?
CY: Be Aware and Alter: To be aware of the karmic or Samskaric patterns that can have a profound influence on your business, while also being aware of the regular work you delegate as a CEO. Keep sharpening your intuition with whatever tools that you can bring up—whether it is *Prathyahara* (moving from being a participant to that of an observer and finally being a witness) or *Dharana* (bringing the mind to focus) or *Dhyana* (meditation or the ability to remain in one thought for a long time). Developing a strong sense of awareness is very important—which most corporates and employees lack. Awareness can take many dimensions. Take the simple example of an employee who is deeply aware of corporate ethics; he will question the 'how' and 'why' of an activity or strategy that his organisation has planned to undertake, to ensure there is no violation of the ethics. Such awareness can protect the brand and reputation of the company and also act as a catalyst for the company's growth. An employee with a still mind, who is unwavering and tranquil, will be an exemplar of a person who will be amenable to developing this awareness.

Accept and Adapt is the next step. Either by allowing the effect to be averted or by predicting the effects (based on the causes you already brought about) or working on correcting the probable cause, one might be able to alter the trajectory to its right course. If the trajectory can't be altered, the best option will be to accept, in a cheerful mood, whatever is in store and move on. In the corporate world, many versatile leaders, managers and employees who tend to be go-getters, frown at the idea of acceptance and treat it as a sign of defeatism (an example of such a situation is the loss of a large deal to a rival competitor). They fail to realise that this antipathy to a healthy mindset will result in a dip in overall team morale and adversely affect the future growth of the business. The ability to practice acceptance, on the other hand, and then learn from the situation/failure will provide a new sense of freedom to achieve bigger successes.

The culmination, always, is about adaptability.

Can you elaborate a bit on adaptability?

CY: I think of it as an Adaptability Quotient or AQ. AQ = (IQ + EQ + SQ + a bit more), where IQ is Intelligence Quotient; EQ is Emotional Quotient and SQ is Spiritual Quotient. The 'bit more' is the unseen element that is still developing and not yet fully understood or comprehended by humans. Those who survive and grow are the ones who most accurately perceive their environment and successfully adapt to it. This involves continuous recalibration of yourself to the external world, i.e., your ability to adjust your internal world to the external world and not vice versa. In our struggle for individual supremacy, we tend to gloss over this aspect and deceive ourselves into thinking that we can manage the external world with our internal capabilities.

This is grossly wrong and history has repeatedly proven that one individual's ego can cause the debacle, not only of that individual but also of the entire clan he was leading. One can look at numerous history and management books, umpteen examples abound to prove this hypothesis. We are mere specks of dust in the overall scheme of things; species of lesser intelligence than us learn to adapt much faster than we humans do. A deadly combination of ego, perceived superior intellect and fragile emotions has caused the downfall of several kingdoms and corporate empires. Traditionally, the business world focussed a lot on IQ as the measure of an individual's success. As time evolved, the truism about EQ playing an equally important role has come to be widely appreciated, paving the way for managers and employees to integrate, collaborate and lead each other effectively.

The Spiritual Quotient, a relatively newer addition, is now being seen as a very important component of success—so leaders are making decisions setting aside their ego and picking what is right from an economical, moral and ethical perspective.

Okay, I get the hang of it. I want to move on to some rapid-fire Q&A rounds. Are you ready Yogi?
CY: Of course.

Rapid-fire Q&A on 'What is your Korporate Karma'?

Can you explain karma in the corporate context, with an example?
Let me start with a quote about this.

> *People should not be thinking about 'making money' but to 'make meaning' or make sense, make a difference, change the world, helping people—and with that they will make money too.*
>
> – Guy Kawasaki, American entrepreneur and investor

Korporate Karma is the concept of action or deed understood as that which causes the entire cycle of cause and effect. It is also seen as the total effect of a person's actions and conduct during successive phases of one's existence. It is a distinctive feeling, aura or the idea that one reaps what one sows—destiny; fate. It's the effects of all actions which are viewed as actively shaping one's past, present and future experiences. It applies as much to a group of individuals as well. In an organisational setup we can't remain unaffected by the individual or collective actions of other members within a group. As in personal life, in corporate life too, the karma of a group can take on a life of its own after years or decades of actions and reactions of individual members of the group.

Korporate Karma invokes many elements, ranging from destiny to deeds, work and actions. It connects the present to your future, whilst also being influenced by your past. Yet, there is a cause-effect mechanism, where our intentions and actions are strongly bound together to affect our future appropriately. Every action you take as an employee or employer, irrespective of your designation, position, team size has a ripple effect on your team and organisation—even the tiniest, most insignificant action. If you do a good job and work hard, you create good karma. If all you think about at work is when you can leave, you are creating bad karma. In many ways, Karma is self-inflicted and influenced by three key factors—Intention, Action and Awareness. In short, knowing, thinking and doing—bearing in mind that everything has an effect and in turn creates more 'causes'.

In the cut-throat corporate culture, what can we do to install 'good karma' thinking?

By orchestrating a positive work culture where there is abundant respect and mutual trust among individuals who constitute the organisation. This will contribute to a healthy workplace emanating positive vibes and subsequently lead to good karma being generated. Organisations have to make a concerted effort to raise the 'Spiritual Quotient' of their employees. Managers and leaders will need to make it a point to recognise and reward employees doing well in this regard to serve as a motivator.

What strategies can businesses undertake to demonstrate their corporate social responsibility (CSR)?

Charity begins at home. The TBL or triple bottom line that organisations want to focus on these days has the 'people' as one of its three fulcrums. The best CSR is to extend a touch of personal care to your people, mould and nurture them into great humans and not just stop at grooming them as productivity machines alone. Corporate governance should focus on maintaining good karma as well. Organisations that tend to be pigeon-holed on short-term profits only, tend to keep CSR as pure 'wall-hanger' statements—nice to display but rarely followed. If businesses can ingrain CSR as an integral part of commitments to their employees, they will make a substantial difference, in the long run.

Business is all about beating our competition. What is the karmic perspective on this?

It is not about the beating competition but beating yourselves and excelling in your lead indicators. As long as you keep the 'karmic race' within the organisation, it will serve you good. Let the competition worry about themselves and their own Korporate Karma. In addition, if organisations adopt a long-term view, then the focus will be less about defeating the competition and more about doing the right thing for the customer, society and world at large.

Can good Korporate Karma translate to superior performance?

It is from a clear conscience that the best performances stem. When the Pandavas engaged in the epic war that lasted eighteen days, their objective was not merely to eliminate the enemies but to reinstate Dharma. Supported and strengthened by such a high objective, they turned out to be a formidable force on the battlefield and embraced victory in the end.

Doing good Korporate Karma translates into maintaining a pure and clear conscience which will, in the long run, translate into superior performance as well. Many companies opted for shortcuts to achieve near term objectives—only to go bankrupt and lose face with their investors, customers and employees. Companies that keep their conscience refined and clear and opt for the path of righteousness will be the ones with the potential to achieve their goals and win accolades.

In times of crisis, what can a leader do to instil continued focus on ethics?
You don't wait for a crisis to happen to instil or focus on ethics. The blue book of any organisation must be built on a sound foundation, which starts with the definition of the DNA of the organisation; what they will stand for at any cost. Once that is done, and inculcated as value systems across the organisation, there is no separate need to focus on ethics. Ethics will then not be an afterthought; it will remain ingrained in the very fabric of the organisation; something every employee fundamentally believes in. It becomes the only prism through which one views the world and in some ways, it builds resilience sufficient enough for the organisation to tide over any crisis.

What strategies and techniques would you recommend so that the concept of 'doing the right thing and doing good' reaches the lowest rung of the employee ladder?
Getting your DNA right; communicating it consistently; allowing people to learn and internalise those DNA values and rewarding them consistently and creating an ambient atmosphere for them to demonstrate it. One thing you will surely notice from the 'best places to work' lists is the undying focus they have on the core values of the organisation. Establishing the right set of motivators and measurement criteria becomes important in encouraging employees to do the right thing.

Given that business is all about measurement, how to measure the effectiveness of a 'Good Karma' initiative?
'Good Karma' initiatives are 'lead indicators' and not 'lag indicators'. If the lead indicators are defined well and as measurable inputs, effectiveness or 'lag indicators' will happen along the way, for sure. Imagine a corporate boardroom, a quarterly business review, etc., where these 'lead indicators' are prominently displayed and quizzed on—every team will then begin to actively incorporate these and aim for success.

Are there examples of 'Korporate Karma' working well in mid- to large-sized companies? If so, can you share some examples?
It is not a conscious decision that many organisations take to define and stick to 'Korporate Karma', as it is still an evolving concept. But by simply looking at the increasing focus on corporate governance, DNA and value-driven leadership initiatives across boardroom and CEO levels in several organisations across the globe, one can gather that Korporate Karma is at work. Today, even spiritual leaders are brought in to the business place to provide advice on matters of leadership. As this trend catches up, every company will take this to heart and make each employee a first-class citizen.

As a CEO, how should I lead by example in this area?
When it comes to values that drive good karma versus output (lead versus lag), the CEO must consistently demonstrate his preference for good karma or values over performance. People don't do as you say; they do as you do. Walk the talk is the mantra for all CEOs. Be what you say and say what you want others to be.

Looking Glass—What is your Korporate Karma?

Key Takeaways:

» Lag indicators are your *effects*, whereas the lead indicators are your *causes*.

» The mind thinks, whereas the heart experiences. All our learning happens through the heart though we are rarely able to accept it.

» We have to be careful of what we sow through our thoughts, deeds and actions.

» In general—it is not the 'what' but the 'how' and the 'why' that matter more.

» Situation handling framework—Raise awareness, alter or accept the situation and adapt to the evolving need.

Action Points:

- » Establish two to three values that are core to your company's vision.
- » Identify lead indicators that align with your company's DNA.
- » Organise awareness sessions on Korporate Karma for your top leaders.
- » Determine the three things that you, as a leader, will do in the next sixty days to inspire your team to do good karma.
- » Brainstorm two scenarios from the recent past that you or your organisation would handle/do differently, based on your new value system.

2

Spiritual Alchemy
The Quintessential Formula

pitaahamasya jagato maataa dhaataa pitaamaha
vedyam pavitramomkaara riksaam yajureva cha | |

I am the father, mother, grandfather of this universe. I am what is to be known; I am the purifier; I am the syllable Om and the Rig, Saama and Yajur Vedas.

| | Gita Ch.9-V.17 | |

Vishnu, the God of Preservation

The Hindu Trinity of gods, Brahma, Vishnu and Shiva, is believed to represent the three phases of cosmic existence—Creation, Preservation and Destruction. Vishnu is believed to be in charge of the protection and sustenance of the universe, by upholding the divine laws of the universe.

His ornate form is depicted in a pleasing sky-blue colour that symbolises His infinite power, and with characteristic embellishments: a lotus to represent purity, a conch shell to stand for the sacred sound, a mace to denote strength, and a chakra that symbolises the mind and the end of self-delusion. Images of Vishnu show Him amidst the vast ocean, with His consort Goddess Lakshmi—who symbolises beauty and wealth—by His side, and resting upon a hundred-headed cobra that represents the many desires of the mind.

He is believed to have incarnated on earth nine times on divine missions to destroy evil and protect the righteous. All through the incarnations, He has manifested Himself in different forms; as Matsya (fish), Koorma (tortoise), Varaha (boar), Narasimha (lion-man), Vamana (dwarf), Parashurama (warrior), Rama (The Idealist) and Krishna (The Endearing Flautist).

Krishna is said to be the only incarnation of Vishnu who was aware of His inherent divine powers from infancy. For this reason, Krishna is considered as Vishnu Himself, rather than being referred to as an incarnation.

Kalki Avatar, on a mission to destroy evil and establish normalcy in Kali Yuga, has been prophesied as the tenth incarnation of Lord Vishnu and is yet to arrive.

As Corporate Yogi was explaining the magnificence of Lord Vishnu and His avatars, my head was swarming with myriad questions. I was amused that it was more or less an enactment of my favourite comic-series from childhood, 'Vikram and Betaal'; a never-ending battle of wits!

I pulled the Yogi into the Q&A session straight away.

Yogi, what are you conveying through the narrative about Lord Vishnu and His avatars? The victory of good over evil, am I right?'

CY: While that is obvious and very much true, I would like to look at each avatar from a deeper level of understanding. The Lord was metamorphosing from one form to the other; Fish > Tortoise > Boar > Lion-Man > Dwarf > Warrior > Ideal-Man (Rama) > God-in-Human-Form (Krishna). Within the scope of each avatar, as and when the situation warranted, He was transforming into better versions of Himself, till the divine mission ordained to Him was completed. You may call it what you like, 'victory of good over evil' or 'beating the competition'. Did you notice that in subsequent avatars, He did not carry even the remotest resemblance to His previous avatars, and instead, came back as entirely different and evolved versions of the value chain?

What is the learning for a CEO in this? Are you suggesting something like 'Kaizen'?

CY: You are bang on target. But at the human level, it assumes greater significance. First, let us get this straight: What is transformation and metamorphosis? Both are suggestive of a trend towards development to higher stages, but with a distinct difference. Transformation is a continuum that keeps happening in a structured manner, within a particular ambit of awareness/activity/grade levels, and culminates at the highest point or peak, but only within the ambit of those levels. Metamorphosis is a leap to an ambit of heightened awareness/activity/grade levels—a quantum leap to the higher evolutionary stage—a paradigm shift.

If we study the process of metamorphosis, we will arrive at a very subtle culmination point known as 'spiritual alchemy'. This is integrated within the process of metamorphosis and it is the highest evolutionary point that completes the process of metamorphosis. Without blending and merging into this most subtle point of inner awareness, metamorphosis will remain partially complete. Without the presence of a Spiritual Alchemist, metamorphosis will be left with a void.

For instance, a junior executive becoming a senior executive, going on to become a manager and then finally a CEO, is just a transformation process; a ubiquitous process along the ladder of promotion. A much deeper approach reveals that a junior executive becoming a better junior executive is a change management process; whereas a junior executive becoming a CEO is a transformation process. Finally, a CEO who remains a CEO still remains a part of the same value chain process.

Can you explain this?

CY: For example, we all know that the lifecycle of a butterfly goes through a 'complete metamorphosis' involving four different stages, egg, larva, pupa and adult; the changes and transformations occur within each one of these stages, but the end result is a complete metamorphosis, without which they may not turn out to be exquisite winged beauties.

A parallel analogy can be drawn from Abraham Maslow's famous theory of Hierarchy of Needs, namely physiological needs (Level 1), safety needs (Level 2), love and belonging (Level 3), esteem needs (Level 4) and self-actualisation (Level 5). Based on this theory, you have the choice of stagnating at any one of the first four levels and never make it to Level 5; or you can excel at a particular level and reach the peak within that level and just stagnate there. You can be at the physiological needs level, or move up to safety needs, then on to love and belonging needs, then on to esteem needs and then, if you are competent and dynamic enough, transform out of these four and metamorphose into the fifth level, of self-actualisation. There are actually very few people, CEOs included, who are able to move up this value chain and seriously and sincerely look at self-actualisation needs.

How does it relate to the significance of the nine avatars?

CY: Every time Vishnu incarnated on a divine mission, He came metamorphosed into a version superior to His previous one. Lord Krishna, the ninth of the avatars, was known as Purana Avatar or 'complete avatar' since He was not only a collective embodiment of all the qualities of the previous eight avatars, but was also considered as a 'realised self in human form'. He was aware of the infinite power inherent in Him and was always ready to exhibit a life of superhuman potentialities.

Similarly, a CEO has enormous potential and he only needs to realise it to bring out the best in himself; not by sticking to the basic management jargon, restricting himself to financials, boardrooms etc. The way Lord Rama, an exemplar of an ideal human being, metamorphosed into the multifaceted Lord Krishna, a CEO has to strive to project the best version of himself and not just be complacent and happy to play within the corridors of power, money, fame etc. As Lord Krishna might say 'It is for mere mortals, Arjuna!'

What do you think a CEO should metamorphose into?
CY: Every human being is potentially divine. Note my words, *potentially*. They need to actualise it. Humans have unimaginable positive potential but rarely will you find someone in that league who has unleashed his full and true potential.

If a CEO is to do full justice to his prestigious position, there are a few essential self-developmental steps that he needs to focus on. Do some soul searching, some self-analysis and self-introspection and identify, if any, the negative human tendencies of avarice, contempt, jealousy, and anger that reside within so you can try to free yourself from its shackles. You have to refine, reprogramme and metamorphose into a lucid personality reflecting the high values and virtues of compassion, and empathy. Equipped with a benevolent disposition and a broader vision, such a leader will be able to allow, to everyone around him, enough freedom to invent opportunities to tap into their true potential and excel in their own ways.

Wouldn't that be counterproductive to an organisation's financial interests?
CY: In fact, the contra will prove to become true. By being aware of the pitfalls of boardroom politics, he would be able to set a benchmark of being a visionary, a people's person, a charismatic leader worthy of emulating. Before you realise, a miracle would happen, the way it happened for the Pandavas with Lord Krishna. Financials (top line, bottom line etc.) are a given on this path when a CEO metamorphoses into his potential self. He moves from the basic instinct of survival to the human instinct of domination to the divine instinct of larger good; and like Lord Krishna, his mere presence as an inspirational figure and visionary, will motivate the men around him to bring out the best in themselves.

Is metamorphosis practically possible in a corporate world of unpredictability?
CY: If you move out of the conditioned approach of the boardroom and corporate organisations and explore the field of human possibilities, you will find that everything has been and can be made possible. Take all the great personalities who have made an indelible mark in the history of the world; great men of science and various other fields, all served as catalysts for the enormous development of the world. Naming a few from the recent past—had it not been for an Einstein, a Mahatma Gandhi, a Swami Vivekananda, a Nelson Mandela, a Mother Teresa, a Dr. Abdul Kalam, amidst us, imagine how much the poorer humanity would have been? What do you think made these seemingly ordinary people, living a typical life as all others, engrave their names in the annals of history? Something made them stand out as special personalities—and it is that element that made all the difference we are talking about.

When we restrict our vision to market share, EPS (earnings per share) and other such things, we remain in the same rut as the others, denying ourselves the freedom to move out of it all and find a better version of us.

Is there a shortcut available for a CEO to move to the next level?
CY: Giving full credit to the CEOs, I would say they have all the prerequisites—versatility, dynamism and effectiveness—to comprehend and move up the value chain. But what they may be lacking is a 'sounding board'. Someone has to come forward to sound the alarm to awaken the CEOs from their slumber and also make them see beyond their current world view.

Do you agree that we had our grandparents being our sounding boards all the time at our homes when we were young? When we grew up and moved out of their direct gaze, haven't we felt a few times that such an imposing yet loving presence was what we needed, to give us a reality check on ourselves, once in a while? You will always find that seasoned CEOs who are not happy or contented with what they are, have more than one sounding board to help them consistently move up the value chain.

Can you tell me a little more about Spiritual Alchemy?
CY: Spiritual Alchemy is defined as the process of taking something ordinary and turning it into something extraordinary; sometimes in a way that cannot be explained. An example of alchemy is, when a person takes a pile of scrap metal and turns it into beautiful art. Let us assume the scrap metal is at the lowest end of the spectrum and the beautiful art is at the higher end of the spectrum; that brings in the three-fold work for an alchemist: change, transform and metamorphose. Spiritual Alchemy is the culmination point embedded within the process of metamorphosis; when the inner awareness reaches a highly refined state and the subtle character traits of the human psyche evolve into a state of pristine purity, the culmination point. A person, basically raw and rough-around-the-edges, getting changed into a refined human being, is brought about by the process of transformation; and a refined human being getting metamorphosed not only into a highly intelligent and effective personality, but also into a highly evolved human being with divine qualities, is the quintessential formula of Spiritual Alchemy.

This is exactly what the CEO should aim to do to himself and to those around him—transform into a refined human being and then metamorphose into a human being with divine qualities. Every human being has the potential, and the need of the hour is to channelise the potential, to attain the highest level of self-actualisation; when this is combined with introspection and internalisation, the Spiritual Alchemist's dream is fulfilled.

Are there any tangible benefits to the organisation in this process?
CY: Of course, there are plenty, financials included. Albert Einstein becoming a renowned scientist from being a simple clerk at a patent office; Mahatma Gandhi, a practising barrister, spearheading a nation's independence; Narendra Modi rising to become the much-applauded prime minister of a vast nation from the simple position of a chai wala—all are examples of mere mortals

transforming and metamorphosing into extraordinary individuals. Each one metamorphosed into their finest versions and inspired several to transform themselves too.

May we move to the rapid-fire Q&A round, Yogi?
CY: Can't wait for it...

Rapid Fire Q&A on 'Spiritual Alchemy—The Quintessential Formula'

Are there many phases and steps to the Spiritual Alchemy of an individual?
Yes. I would rather say it is a lifelong process; a process of constant learning, unlearning and relearning. You also have to bear in mind that there is no tailor-made, one-size-fits-all approach. Each individual has to chart out their own path and work on themselves.

How do we focus on influencing the transformation of a team, division and organisation?
It starts with the work of mapping and finding the true potential of each individual. It has to be a combined effort by the concerned individual, his superiors and peers; and with liberal support and encouragement from the organisation to the individual to move up the value chain. It is a long-term game and organisations should not work with short term ROIs (returns on investment) alone in mind.

Ego as a positive force is the motivating factor behind the success of individuals as well as companies. How can we ensure that we use ego positively and effectively?
Ego is the force multiplier, both in negative and positive ways. Ego is nothing but a bundle of energy. If the CEO learns to temper his ego with spiritual wisdom, his ego can, in fact, become a positive force multiplier of the highest order. Wisdom lies in acknowledging and accepting the fact that you are just a part of the whole and not the whole by yourself. When we operate in all areas of life keeping the larger picture in mind, whatever we do turns out to be the right thing.

How to delegate without fear (in a spirit of detachment and letting go) and reduce my sense of insecurity?

Korporate Karma works on Input (Efforts or lead indicators) rather than output (Results or lag indicators). Focus on delegating/ sharing more of 'efforts or lead indicators' rather than focussing on 'results or lag indicators'. This way the person you are delegating wouldn't have to have the pressure of 'results' on him/her. To that extent it makes it easier on him/her to accept the task that is delegated.

What can be done so teams or individuals don't feel hindered by negativities like self-doubt or pride?

When a person is on a journey of self-discovery, he would be so preoccupied with his progress that he will find himself with very little time for such negative factors. The key is to create a perfect balance of perpetual self-discovery, moving towards self-actualisation. Periodical 360-degree feedback also goes a long way in keeping people grounded. Keep challenging your team members in a positive sense and create a platform of trust and respect across the organisation, making them feel like they're a part of an extended family.

At times, co-workers can hold past grudges against each other. Can qualities such as forgiveness be instilled and, if so, how?

Well regulated 'hot-seat' sessions are a good way to get over this kind of resentment between colleagues, along with the right dosage of enabling forgiveness. A hot-seat session is where a person takes a seat and just listens to everything shared about him from all his peers and team members. He is not permitted to respond, but he can ask clarifying questions to understand the intent behind the feedback.

It is said that the transformation of an individual can lead to changes of teams/divisions at large. Is this a pipe dream or something that can be achieved?

Change is the precursor to transformation. With the right type of nudging and periodical training, people can be better prepared to improve their AQ (Adaptability Quotient).

Have we seen specific metrics on the measurement of organisational/ individual transformations?
While results will speak for themselves, the metrics that we need to draw here will be for lead indicators (input or efforts) and not lag indicators (output or results).

Are there good examples of 'Spiritual Alchemy' at work in contemporary times?
Every compassionate leader provides a perfect platform for Spiritual Alchemy to take place. If you look back at your own career, you will find innumerable examples of such leaders; not just in contemporary times, but even in the last few decades.

Though it might go under different names, there are several case studies for Spiritual Alchemy at the workplace. If you look at any of the 'great places to work' organisations, you will find a distinct cultural shift that makes Spiritual Alchemy happen. At a Global Level, Unilever, Oprah Winfrey Network, Aflac are a few organisations where these concepts are practised consciously. In India, we have read stories of the effect of Ramakrishna Paramahamsa on Vivekananda and how he set up the Mutt in a big way. Heartfulness Institute has several case studies where they have helped organisations transform using these principles. If we scrutinise many small and medium-sized organisations, you will invariably find the silent transformation that is taking place, though these are not always documented.

Looking Glass—Spiritual Alchemy—The Quintessential Formula

Key Takeaways:

» Alchemy can be of two kinds—One is change management, where an individual/organisation strives to be a better version of themselves and the second is where an individual takes a transformative leap relative to their existing role.

» A CEO/leader ought to aim to drop the shackles of negative human tendencies and metamorphose himself into a person of empathy—thereby motivating his team members to live to their full potential too.
» Spiritual Alchemy is a long-term play for an organisation, wherein metamorphosis is happening at a different pace for varying individuals within the company.
» Lord Krishna demonstrated leadership by influence as a viable strategy—without firing a single arrow. He led men to victory on the battlefield with vision, acumen, compassion and supra-human qualities.
» A CEO who can rise above the beaten track of merely focussing on financials or bottom line, will motivate and inspire individuals, teams and organisations to envision a better version of themselves.

Action Points:

» Identify two individuals in your executive circle who can act as sounding boards for you as a CEO/leader. Replicate this with your top leadership and encourage them to find mentors as well.
» Organise hot-seat sessions for your key leaders and employees and ask them to play back what they have heard in terms of feedback (without getting judgmental).
» Nominate a few of your leaders to become 'Spiritual Alchemy' champions so they can drive transformative behaviour across teams.
» Introspect as a CEO and identify the top three negative behaviours that you would like to change over the next one year.
» Establish an incentive programme to recognize top performers who have driven Spiritual Alchemy initiatives.

3

Cause and Effect
Where is Your Focus?

ye tu dharmyaamritamidam yathoktam paryupaasate
shradyadhaanaa matparamaa bhaktosteteeva me priyaha||

Those who follow this path that is in keeping with dharma, with a mind full of faith in Me, and for whom I am their supreme goal, those devotees are exceedingly dear to Me.

|| Gita Ch.12-V.20 ||

Bhakta Prahlad

Hiranyakasipu, a demon king who ruled the three worlds, abhorred Lord Vishnu for having killed his brother Hiranyaksha in his Varaha Avatar. The demon king ordered the sages and celestials to worship him instead of Lord Vishnu as God, and those who disobeyed were harassed and punished and their yagnas destroyed. The tormented rishis, along with Brahma, sought refuge under Lord Vishnu, narrating their tale of woes. The time had come for Lord Vishnu's next avatar.

Hiranyakasipu's wife was an ardent devotee of Lord Vishnu. She used to hear hymns in praise of Lord Vishnu and her unborn son, Prahlada, also heard them when he was still in her womb. He grew up into a devout young boy and was duly initiated into Gurukula.

He kept singing the glories of Lord Vishnu and encouraged the other boys too to emulate him. On hearing this, Hiranyakasipu was furious and ordered the boy to be tortured till he mended his ways. Lord Vishnu protected the boy from all the harrowing experiences. Prahlada remained unshakeable in his faith, much to the chagrin of his father. Frustrated, Hiranyakasipu asked Prahlada 'Where is your Lord Vishnu?'

'Everywhere,' Prahlada said.

'Inside this pillar too?' he asked.

'Yes,' replied Prahlada.

Blind with rage, Hiranyakasipu slammed the pillar with his mace and Narasimha, in his frightening form of half-lion and half-man, emerged with a roar. With Hiranyakasipu immobilised in His lap, Narasimha sat on the threshold of the building, and tore the body of the demon king with His sharp fingers. To evade death, Hiranyakasipu had received a boon from Brahma, according to which he could only be killed when it was neither day nor night, neither inside not outside, and by neither a man nor an animal. The tyranny ended and Prahlada inherited the throne and remained a devout and righteous ruler.

As soon as Yogi finished the Puranik story, I straight away got into the session with the first question:

How does this story connect with a CEO's life?

CY: If you look at it, the character traits of Hiranyakasipu and Prahlada are in stark contrast to one another. Given his ideas of conquering the entire cosmic universe and proclaiming himself God, the father was obviously working on end results or effects. In contrast, the son, Prahlada, was working on cause, knowing well who the true lord was. While Hiranyakasipu was frenetically trying to expand his territorial monarchy and meting out punishments to those who didn't accept him as the supreme lord (it is fine if this reminds you of corporate situations), Prahlada was busy creating a promising future for himself by working on cause.

You recall lag versus lead indicators? The message a CEO can discern from this Puranic episode, is to either choose to concentrate on control and results or focus on making the cause work for him (similar to Prahlada being protected from all harm by Vishnu, the Cause of everything). The 'why and how' should take precedence over the 'what'. Hiranyakasipu had to go through strenuous penance to become worthy of receiving the boon as a special reward, but the blunder that caused the tides to turn against him was when he tried to exercise his control over the source of the boon itself.

If Hiranyakasipu had learnt from his botched attempts at punishing his own son and tried to atone for the sins he had committed, he would have turned towards Lord Vishnu and got himself endeared to Him, as he had been prior to receiving the boon. Instead, all he was doing was sinking deeper in the cesspool, blinded by his senseless fury.

Can you elaborate on this idea, sharing some insights from a corporate situation?

CY: I intend to do that myself. In the corporate world, we can find many examples where individuals/managers, aiming to grab more turf, engage in kingdom-building activities and find themselves inexplicably caught in the interplay of office politics. If they can ask 'why' when such things pop-up, it will give them a way to solve these proactively instead of being drawn into such negativities. Instead, what is disheartening is to find them focussing too much on 'what'; they tend to point the finger at a colleague's fault or put the other team into a comparison trap, and try to project themselves as a cut above the rest.

The concept of discrimination is an important factor in decision-making and problem-solving and we can see that employees rarely spend time on introspection and development of discriminative intelligence. Man is endowed with the greatest intellectual faculty called 'Viveka' or the ability to discriminate. This ability is not to just discriminate between good and bad, right and wrong etc. but to explore beyond those limitations. True Viveka enables one to differentiate between cause and effect. At every stage in life, you will have the ability to make a choice, considering the situational factors. Every choice creates a set of consequences that follow and once the choice is made, it is next to impossible to reverse or manipulate the impending outcome, as the choice is on its way to getting executed or manifested—strategise and execute, to use corporate parlance. The best choices come from the best questions. As Voltaire would say, 'Judge a man by his questions rather than by his answers.'

What kind of questions do you suggest?

CY: Before I speak about the kind of questions—I hasten to add, it is also important for the CEO and leaders to create an open environment where everyone feels free to ask the right questions. To ensure CEOs of high-growth companies get the optimum results they are hired for, it is imperative to spend at least a third of their time thinking about business strategy, making adjustments, taking calculated risks, and communicating these decisions throughout the organisation. This kind of structured strategic planning should become a norm and must be diligently followed by CEOs, even in some of their day-to-day activities, by deciphering what will 'cause' the 'effect'. The questions they need to ask to get the required result would have to cover a wide range of possibilities, whether they are karmic based or management-related.

Karmic questions could cover points such as: 'how to make people think positively to build positive karma'; 'how should I be treating my team members'; 'how to build a culture of positive conscience to take the organisation through its chartered path', etc. Management questions could deal with points like: 'why do I want the result that I am aiming for or have been asked to aim for'; 'why should my team cooperate with me to reach the goals that are laid out for the organisation', and so on.

Would such questions be achievement-oriented?

CY: These questions will bring forth the right answers and the answers will contribute to recalibrating the values and standards of the organisation. Values establish a company's identity and behaviour. They should help to propel the business forward; otherwise, they will become nonessential for the future. To retain the intrinsic value of the 'values', it is important to live the values. Standards are about expectations, they guide our decisions, and they are also the measuring stick for values. CEOs are directly responsible for setting the standards and ethics of an organisation and they are seen as the role models who could either lead or mislead, depending on how oriented and value-driven they are. The values, standards and ethics ingrained in the organisation help in balancing sufficient yield in the present with necessary investment in the future, people being the organisation's most valuable asset.

Questions also help CEOs understand how to balance the outside and the inside; the outside here can mean all that is external to the organisation or external to the CEO himself, while the inside can be taken as the core of the organisation or the CEO's persona.

Will the questions serve any other additional purposes?

CY: Of course. The 'why and how' questions specifically will help you to make substantial discoveries. They will help reveal conflicts and change those results that are not beneficial to you in every area of your life. The 'why' question, on the other hand, exposes the underlying purpose in 'why something exists' or 'why it is done'. It is an essential element of any growth-oriented approach in life and a tool for decluttering the mind. If you do what you have always done, you will get what you have always got. Instead, when you get yourself to ask the question 'why', every time you embark on a venture, you will involuntarily wait for the answer to appear and shape your next course of action. Of course, the combination of logical and heart-based thinking would lead to a set of answers. If the answers appear logical, then proceed to action phase. Else, move into the 'why' phase again, even with those answers. Like the way you would peel off layers of an onion before reaching its core, you are bound to get the answers to these 'why' questions at some point. A little bit of trial and error implementation with the first set of answers might also reveal if you are on the right track.

When the 'why' question is directed at issues that destabilise the functioning of the world at various levels—those pertaining to imbalances in the global ecosystem, natural calamities like famine, floods, drought, etc.; humanitarian problems like poverty, illiteracy, etc.; animal welfare issues; and socio-economic disparities and many such things—it will create widespread awareness among all and help to redeem and restore the balance in all aspects of life.

Innovative people with grit and determination will confront the 'why' question as often as needed and bring forth concrete results that will move them up the value chain.

For example, an employee who understands the 'why' behind why his company exists will be better aligned to the company's values and deliver better output in the long run, as compared to someone who never stops to understand the 'why'. The 'how', equally important, helps one to navigate towards the cause that will lead to the effect. Leaders who pause to reflect on the 'how' are able to look ahead, plan for the future and lay out a clear roadmap to take things forward. Hence, the path to the cause becomes clear and smooth, and in future if changes need to be made, they can be integrated with a clear sense of purpose.

Shall we move to the rapid-fire Q&A round, Yogi?
CY: Sure, with pleasure.

Rapid-fire Q&A on 'Cause and Effect—Where is Your Focus?'

Is there an effective way to look at past failures and clearly demarcate cause and effect?
Mistakes or failures are not a problem, but not taking the opportunity to learn from them is. Identify your mistakes and learn from them

quickly, focussing on what caused them rather than how to fix the effect temporarily. No point in doing patchwork to get over something in the short run. In every mistake, there is potential for growth. We are products of our past, but we don't have to let our mistakes define us. Failure is the only way to grow yourself and grow your organisation, because ultimately, it is how we learn to succeed. The wisdom of learning from failure is incontrovertible. And yet, organisations that do this well are extraordinarily rare. The attitudes and activities required to to detect and analyse failures effectively are in short supply in most companies, and the need for context-specific learning strategies is underappreciated. If CEOs and leaders focus on creating a culture of working on what 'caused' a failure or a mistake, the organisations will go a long way in their journey of continuous and steady improvement.

As we do a root-cause analysis of unfavourable events caused by individuals, how do we manage people, so they don't take things personally?

Management would be easy if everyone you managed was hard-working, collaborative, and had a great attitude and exceptional talent. But then it wouldn't be management, would it? The reality, of course, is far different. Simply put, some people are easy to manage and others are hard. There is no light switch to flick for immediate solutions to vexing employee problems. But certain fundamental approaches can make the difficult more routine, and can have relevance for employees at all levels—whether you're managing on the shop floor or in the c-suite. My key inputs to this question:

- Have transparent communication.
- Work towards building respect and trust.
- Enable a boundary-less organisation whose culture is focussed on the betterment of a healthier whole.
- Develop a culture of having a team of 'open-minded people'.
- Learn to listen, listen and listen.
- Plan as much as possible to avoid leaving things to chance.

Is there a level of determinism between effects in an organisation and specific corporate actions?

Yes, of course, starting with the mindset of the CEO and people involved. It is not what happens to us but how we respond to it. So, the role of the CEO or his top team is to ensure they set in place predictable processes to create predictable results or outcomes. Deterministic corporate actions create deterministic effects. The key is to be proactive, learn from past mistakes and failures to keep proper checks and balances that can trigger alarms before the building comes collapsing down on you! The other important aspect is to institute a culture where we don't punish employees who take risks and who may fail (all within ethical boundaries). Employees and teams contribute fearlessly.

How can we influence individuals and organisations to develop an awareness of the consequences of actions (good and bad)?

How did we learn the difference between good and bad? We were taught by our parents and teachers when we were young and we also learnt by observing and aping a bit. Of course, good or bad is part of one's belief system and can change from one person to the next. Continuous education is necessary to maintain a uniform culture of right and wrong (in corporate parlance, it is better to rephrase as right and wrong instead of good and bad). Same as the case with Prahlada! He was taught in his Gurukul the difference between good and evil and he took the side of good. It was ingrained in him by the time he grew up. He also had peers around him who were vibrating in the same thought frequency. The same is true for corporate life too. If we can set up the right motivations, individuals will gravitate towards the right actions. If a few team members do the right thing, it also motivates others to go in that direction.

How can I draw insights and see a signal amidst noise and chaos?

It is the design of nature for order to arise from chaos. Look at the world around you and observe. At every moment there is an element of chaos, but order soon returns. As the Buddha might say, 'Wait patiently; still your mind' and the situation shall become clearer once things settle down. A calm mind is a precursor to clear thinking. One can practice meditation or any mind silencing technique, which can yield instant and immediate results when mastered sufficiently. In addition, this also goes into the discussion of the company's values and beliefs. A strong sense of purpose can guide leaders through the noise and chaos.

What can we do to instil proactiveness in teams—to ensure they predict and arrest unfavourable outcomes before they occur?
There are several ways to do this but let me share something simple. It starts with building awareness of expectations and communicating measurable results frequently, and having frequent conversations proactively. Understand what motivates each one of your team members. Move towards a collaborative working model where each one feeds on one another's knowledge, experience and success (or failure). Continue to work on their skill building while working on project outcomes and results. And develop future leaders early by developing deep talent pools so that your team members see the bigger picture of organic growth.

Creative minds in an organisation drive innovation. How do we ensure focus and alignment to the corporate direction of profitability?
In the first place, the organisation must have an innovation culture in place. People must be encouraged to take risks, and be supported if and when they fail. In parallel, tie compensation to performance and reward creative ideas which produce results (either in the short term or long term). This is what changes behaviour. Please don't penalise mistakes. People aren't willing to experiment when they are afraid. Ensure you embrace leaders who are ready to take positive risks to bring about creative outcomes. In addition, innovative minds need to be provided space to have the freedom to create at will; therefore, identifying the right initiatives within the company for them is important.

How to put the maximum focus on the cause and accomplish things as the by-product (with the least effort)?

When you go on a thousand-mile journey in your car, how far can you see even if you know the goal? May be 100 to 200 metres, at best? The same is true for our work and work culture as well. While the CEO is clear on the long-term vision and goals for his organisation, his immediate focus should always be on the next 100 to 200 metres that he wants his team to run. That can happen only when the organisation has the habit of 'efforts focus' and not 'results focus'. One or two must be looking at the larger picture of long-term results but not the entire team. The general who takes an army to war knows the result he wants, but his job is to give the day's focus to the soldiers and not burden them with the final result. Of course, the soldiers, too, know what the outcome should be, but they are focussed on the day's efforts at the battlefront. So, you see, the onus is on the CEO or leader to ensure the team puts focus on the efforts and not the results.

How do we challenge resistance to new ideas (cause) that can have unfavourable effects (remaining of status quo)?

Resistance is usually created because of certain blind spots and attitudes that people have due to their preoccupation with the technical aspects of new ideas. It can be taken care of by:

- Proactively handling misunderstanding and lack of trust.
- Continuous communication and education.
- Resolving conflicts quickly and effectively.
- Remaining positive and supportive.

Can spirituality aid in the breaking of the unsavoury cause-effect cycle?

The first step spirituality enables you to take is to understand that the effects were caused by you and no one else. It is all about personal accountability. It is in the thinking and followed by the choices you have made. The theory of Samskaras says that 'choices made in divine thinking' reduce the impact of the effects affecting you. It might be difficult to believe but it is true. Take the story of

Prahlada. All his choices were made in Lord Vishnu's name and he had the backing of the Lord himself at all adverse moments. The logical brain won't be able to process this or accept this but think of it this way: a seed sown on your own and one sown under the guidance of a trained horticulturist will have a whale of a difference.

There is a logical way of looking at it too. How I process a situation determines not just how that situation will turn out or the likely chain of events that will follow, but how I will interact with my family and friends, how much energy I will have for my work, how motivated I will be to read and do my piano practice, etc. Everything in my life is affected by how I deal with my thoughts and subsequent emotions and feelings. This is the law of cause and effect for a logical mind. Again, it boils down to your thinking and the conscious choices you make.

Looking Glass—Cause and Effect—Where is Your Focus?

Key Takeaways:

- Understanding and working towards the cause is important.
- Ability to discriminate is an important leadership attribute.
- The right questions shape the value and standards of the organisation.
- 'Why' and 'how' are important to introspect in critical situations.
- Spirituality can be a good aid to break the 'cause-effect' cycle.

Action Points:

- Design an internal campaign around raising deep awareness of company values and standards.
- Run a focus group/workshop for key leaders around the relationship between cause and effect.
- Institute a reward system for leaders who question and are open.

- » Pilot a spiritual mindset with a few teams to drive changes in cause-effect behaviour.
- » Organise a session around raising awareness about the power of discrimination (remember Viveka—differentiating between right and wrong, cause and effect?) in the corporate world.

4

It is Not Just the Financials Anymore
Corporate TBL and Spiritual TBL

shauryarh tejo dhritir dakhyarh yuddhe chapy apalayanam
danam ishvara-bhavash cha khatram karma svabhava-jam | |

Valour, splendour of personality, resolve, adroitness, fortitude, dauntlessness in battle, generosity and leadership abilities are the naturally endowed duties of a Kshatriya.

| | Gita Ch.18-V.43 | |

Kautilya—The Concept of a King

Monarchy or king's rule was the most accepted system of government in ancient India, right from the Vedic period. The two famous epics of our country, Ramayan and Mahabharata, happened around the time when the monarchical rule was the popular system of government.

Kautilya, also known as Chanakya, the versatile royal advisor during the rule of King Chandragupta of the Maurya dynasty, wrote the *Arthashastra*, an ancient treatise on statecraft, economic policy and military strategy.

Kautilya's elaborate ideologies specifying the requisite skills and attributes that a king should possess were unique and still hold good for successful leaders thousands of years later.

The king was the chief executive and had sovereign authority in the whole system of politics and administration. The safety and security of his kingdom and his subjects were his prime concerns; apart from that, a king should necessarily possess a set of exemplary qualities to promulgate a reign based on the Dharmic code. The king's duties spanned a wide range of activities that called for the embodiment of the high values of morality and ethics, integrity, discipline, eloquence and listening skill.

His stature required him to be physically fit, possess an alert and incisive mind and a high intellect; he must be able to assimilate and contemplate on the profound learnings in various fields, including spirituality and philosophy and be amenable to taking on board the views of erudite scholars, and also have the discriminative intellect to identify and reject unproductive ideas.

Chanakya conjured up such a picture of an ideal king, and the young princes of the royal household were groomed strictly conforming to his guidelines.

As Yogi discussed the topic, 'It is not just the financials anymore—' my mind was filled with questions and I shot off the first one.

Aren't financial principles the only guiding factor for a CEO?

CY: Let me share an interaction with a young executive who asked me a similar question. Instead of giving him a direct answer, I wanted to prise an answer from him through his understanding and asked him a series of related questions.

My first question was 'Young man, let us say, for instance, that you have got all the money you wanted, would that make you happy?'

He said, 'Of course, yes. No doubt about that'.

'Okay, fine. Now that you have all the money you wished for, what would you rather be—a person with good health or one with poor health?'

'Both. Abundant wealth and robust health too,' he replied.

I turned the conversation around and asked, 'What if you had wealth and health, but you were unhappy with your spouse?'

'I would prefer a happy life with my spouse.'

'That is a good way to look at life. All said and done, what if you had a nasty, abusive boss at your workplace?'

I could see he was slowly losing his ground. Uncertainty writ large on his face, he said rather inconclusively, 'I would prefer to quit such a workplace.'

I took it as far as it could go, deeper and deeper with a volley of questions, till the fresh young executive found himself cornered with an array of options to either choose or forego in life.

Inevitably it all points to the example of the cartwheel, which has spokes riveted to a wooden inner hub (also called a core) and a hinge that holds it all together. Which spoke can one afford to give up and yet have the balance maintained in the wheel? What would happen if the hinge gave way but the spokes and other parts are doing well? The hinge here is what one would refer to as 'the soul' or 'the heart', which holds everything together, and yet stays inconspicuous in almost all situations.

The young executive in the above interaction is an illustrative example of many young aspirants who begin by looking at life with a focussing on just one dimension. Even in the general category of people, many individuals live their entire lives with their focus fixed on a single dimension, viz., that of money, only to realise in the evening of their life, that they did not notice the hinge of the cartwheel (the soul) that held their life together.

Many corporate organisations demonstrate a similar short-minded approach in their quest for only one thing—the financials, while a broader perspective is called for.

I allowed the enormity of the message, the simple example narrated above tried to convey, to slowly sink in, before I reeled off my next question.

So, the metaphor is to tell the CEO that there is a lot more to life than just financials?

CY: You can take this book itself as an example. Do you think the publisher will be happy with just the money flowing in from the book's sales? I bet not. Other than the sales numbers it brings in, they would look at a range of other parameters to decide on the success of the book. While there is no doubt that the publisher's primary concern would be to make a substantial margin of profit from the sale of the book, there is also a bigger stake that depends on the impact the book might have on its target audience. If the book appeals to the audience and caters to their requirements in buying it, they would choose to become patrons of the particular publishing house and look to buying more books from them. As against the short-term benefit of realising an immediate profit through sales of the particular book, earning the patronage of the reading fraternity will prove to be more beneficial and stabilising for the publisher, in the long run.

Apart from the financials, what other things does a CEO have to look out for?

CY: A typical response to this question is: it depends on many factors and a multi-dimensional approach has to be adopted.

The working teams will have the following questions invariably running in the back of their minds: a) Who are we as a work team, department, or organisation? b) Is our work worthy? c) What is our greater purpose? d) What are our values and ethical principles? e) What will our legacy be?

To arrive at the right answers to these questions, the CEO must understand the 'new normal' success keys of the twenty-first century.

And what could the answers be?

CY: One of the key components, to begin with, is a vision of the workplace. The spiritual CEO should strive for a workplace that functions truly as a community, consisting of people with shared traditions, values, and beliefs. A workplace where employees feel connected to the company plays a crucial role in delivering optimal results.

While the current crop of business leaders are astute in their understanding and execution of business strategies, ensuring a sustained top line and bottom line for their organisations, there is a gap between what the followers (internal and external) expect from their leaders and what the leaders actually deliver. For the kind of sustainable TBL (triple bottom line) that organisations are seeking to achieve these days (financial, people and society related goals being balanced), there is a great demand on leaders to bring additional dimensions to leadership, hitherto uncommon in the corporate world. The current crop of business leaders need to familiarise themselves with the emerging concepts of spiritual leadership, leading to a practice of the new TBL (a combination of personal spiritual leadership, organisational spiritual leadership and sustainability).

Can you expand on this further, please?

CY: Sure. At the outset, the spiritual leader has to create a workplace for his team that functions as an integrated community with shared values, traditions and beliefs. The multifaceted requirements of dynamic leadership undergo variations and get refined periodically. Still, in general, all standard definitions of wise leadership agree that it involves the ability to exert a positive and healthy influence on the followers. If a leader in the workplace possesses spiritually refined qualities, it gets reflected in his/her mode of functioning, healthy attitude, emotions and behaviour, and it creates the same healthy and positive spirit in the workplace, motivating the subordinates to excel in their work and also pursue a spiritual path in their lives.

On the other hand, if a leader is too self-centred, riding on a huge ego, and has an authoritarian approach, the sub-ordinates may not feel connected to the real purpose of the organisation and work in constant fear of triggering an unpleasant situation. Such an approach by the one at the top may bring in some short-term results but will not be productive in the long run—it will be the proverbial case of missing the forest for the trees.

What do followers expect?

CY: At the fundamental level, followers want to be treated as active partners within the organisation. This means subordinates should be allowed to take an active part in consultations, given due respect and treated like family (where contributions are valued and there is a shared sense of risk and reward). Hence, inculcating and integrating values of spirituality into the vistas of leadership has the potential to infuse much-needed harmony in a workplace and create an environment conducive to handling people and issues in a more humane and compassionate manner. From the subordinates' perspective, such an egalitarian approach will be highly appreciated, and contribute to a sense of shared purpose. From the organisation's perspective, a leadership nourished by spiritual values may lead to greater levels of trust, organisational support, and commitment among employees, which could have tremendous positive effects on organisational performance.

However, spirituality in leadership should not be treated as a superficial 'device' or 'tool' to aid in improved organisational outcomes. Instead, it should be internally assimilated and contemplated upon, with genuine belief to transform, refine and help improve the character traits of the leaders. If application and demonstration of spiritual values are not backed by a spirit of authenticity, the effects created will tend to fade away as just another fad.

Can you tell me the difference between the Old Model and the New Model of TBL?

CY: Look at these two images.

The old model of TBL looks like this:

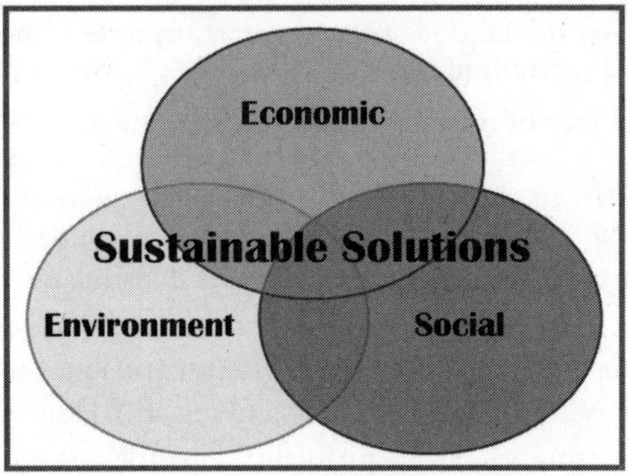

The new model of TBL looks like this:

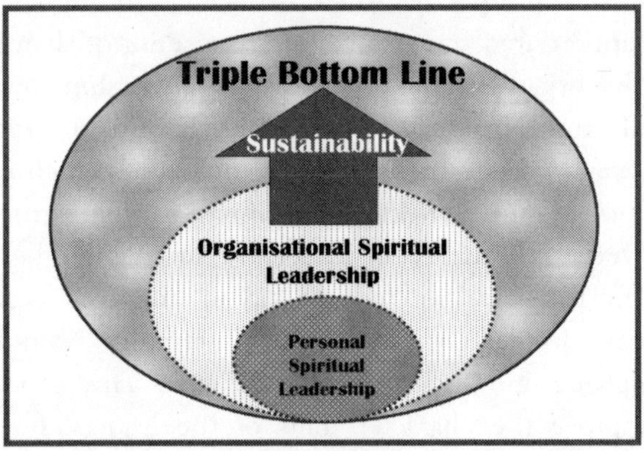

As you can see, in the new TBL model there is a strong emphasis on personal spiritual leadership as the foundation upon which the organisational spiritual leadership is built. A strong foundation like this will weather the storms in the business climate and allow leaders to take business decisions with a spiritual bentof mind.

Thank you. I get it. So, it is imperative on the part of CEOs to rethink their current approach to leadership?

CY: Yes. All this reflects and reiterates an emerging urgent call for leaders to rethink how they live their lives and lead their organisations and provide for the thriving economic success of their organisation. They must move away from the beaten track and carve a new path that accommodates core values like the welfare of employees and society. They must contribute to the development of local and global economies and improved awareness of environmental issues.

Thus, regardless of the status quo, the very definition of leadership, should encapsulate all that goes into building a world that we would want our children and grandchildren to inherit.

Needless to say, a transformation on the above lines is far from easy and cannot happen overnight, but it is high time that CEOs start thinking seriously in this direction and take concrete steps.

May we move to the rapid-fire Q&A round, Yogi?

CY: Sure.

Rapid-fire Q&A on 'It is Not Just the Financials Anymore—Corporate TBL & Spiritual TBL'

Are there good examples of companies who have seen success by focussing on spiritual TBL—beyond the financials?

Quite a few organisations have focussed on Spiritual TBL, though it might be referred to as 'Values' internally. Value is subjective, based on an individual's emotional maturity and perception of the context. Value is not objective, predetermined by an external party and enforced on a community. These days, it is a question that is best answered by perception, as objective measures are still shaping up. If you take the Indian scenario, you have shining examples at the top level of the Tata Group, TVS Group, Godrej Group, Wipro, the Mahindras, CEAT, GHCL, Caparo and many more. If you look at the landscape of startups and MSMEs (Micro, Small and

Medium Enterprises) that I have personally witnessed, there are several that run on positive values, spiritual and otherwise. They are all doing quite well on the financial front too. Examples are important, but even more important is for every leader to design something unique to their DNA or culture.

How can we measure and score high on the mental well-being of employees?
Defining the DNA to include positive and spiritual values, bringing in measures through PMS (Performance Management System), periodical appraisals and feedback is one way this can be achieved.

What kind of programmes can we inculcate within organisations to drive and measure the overall well-being of corporate workers?
In the last few years, organisations have started understanding the value of 'all-round well-being' and are implementing programmes to educate and help employees to feel a sense of oneness with the organisation. Many organisations have 'induction' programmes, at which stage itself they bring in the culture of 'all-round well-being'. This can include physical, mental, emotional and spiritual well-being. We are beginning to see a trend where spiritual institutions are bringing the power of ancient Indian traditions to the corporate marketplace—many of which are quite relevant in the latter.

Can interpersonal relationships in the workplace be improved by embracing spiritual techniques? If so, how?
You must have read about the concept of 'emotional bank account' in the work of the great management thinker Stephen R. Covey. Workplaces have been thinking about and implementing such measures and they are all part of the L&D (learning and development) culture of scores of organisations. Spiritual techniques take the employees (at all levels) towards an all-inclusive culture instead of just looking at mutual financial benefits alone. Making them aware of Korporate Karma and helping them align their beliefs and values while moving towards the financial goals of the organisation, is the first positive step one can take.

How to align karmic P&L with business P&L?
I would rephrase the question to: 'how to align business P&L with karmic P&L'. Since Korporate Karma is what determines the business P&L, I would focus on the input rather than the output. Karma is surely the biggest input we all bring to the table. Every corporate has a certain Korporate Karma that they come with (due to historical events). In addition, Korporate Karma is influenced by the market and other environments at play at that time. Through their everyday actions, every company can influence how Korporate Karma helps or hinders them in their corporate journey.

The concept of focus on a single bottom line tends to be ingrained within an organisation, especially with sales and financial personnel. How do we change this mindset?
You might want to recall the story of the young executive we spoke about at the beginning of this chapter. With Indigo children gaining a definite foothold, we are working with a generation that is more focussed on values than we could ever imagine. (According to a pseudo scientific New Age concept, Indigo children are believed to possess special, unusual, and sometimes supernatural traits or abilities. No scientific studies give credibility to their existence or their attributes as yet; deeper references are there in the book 'Peaceful Parenting' and on the internet as well).

In fact, a change in mindset is needed for those at the top and not for the recruits. Hence, for those at the top, the first step is to develop the right awareness. Gradually, when top leaders can see the long-term benefits, they will align with the new TBL (triple bottom line) model.

If we are in a difficult negotiation with a customer on price—but we know selling at that price could impact the other BLs (bottom lines)—what strategies can we use to convince the customer?
This question is as old as the profession of 'selling' itself! It is the intangibles that take precedence in a sale situation, rather than the tangibles. Price is tangible whereas how a customer feels while

buying is intangible. Ninety per cent weightage can be given to the intangible and ten per cent to the tangible. Isn't that what great brands do? When was the last time you saw a great brand being sold on the price factor?

Does culture and diversity have a role to play in our measurement of the overall bottom line?
It's common for people to pit culture and diversity against excellence and bottom-line performance, as if their interaction is a zero-sum game. But more and more evidence suggest that diverse teams are actually better at reaching their goals. Many studies done in the recent past show a trend of culture and diversity improving bottom line performance significantly. Of course, culture and diversity bring their own set of challenges and that is something the CEO must bear in mind as a trade-off he has to work with. Fortunately, in corporate boardrooms today, there is increased awareness of the role of diversity/culture—so more and more firms are paying attention.

Are there examples of CEOs who have embraced spiritual TBL well?
In the Indian context alone, you have the likes of Azim Premji, Ratan Tata, Shiv Nadar, Adi Godrej, Narayana Murthy and many more. They are luminaries, but remember, you as a leader have the opportunity to create the right version of spiritual TBL relevant for *your* organisation.

***Looking Glass—It is Not Just the Financials Anymore*—Corporate TBL and Spiritual TBL.**

Key Takeaways:

- » The new TBL model has personal/organisational spiritual leadership as the foundation.
- » A Spiritual CEO ought to create a workplace with shared traditions, values and beliefs.
- » Spirituality in leadership has to be grounded in genuine belief on the part of the leaders.

» Korporate Karma determines the business P&L.
» Employees today have expectations from their leaders, which are beyond the financials.

Action Points:

» Organise a workshop with employees to see if their expectations and leadership focus are aligned.
» For the upcoming year, design one additional measurement beyond financials as part of the TBL.
» Articulate or enhance your Vision statement with an eye on Spiritual TBL.
» Engage in a discussion with your top managers on what Korporate Karma means for your organisation.
» Design one programme for employees, focussed on enhancing their overall mental and spiritual well-being.

5

The Korporate DNA
A Place for Shared Traditions, Values and Beliefs

urdhvam gachchhanti sattva-stha madhyeti sthanti rajasah
jaghanya-guna-vritti-stha adho gachchhanti tamasah | |

Those established in the mode of goodness evolve to higher goals; those belonging to the mode of action stay in the mid-course; and those in the mode of ignorance degenerate.

| | Gita Ch.14-V.18 | |

God is Not Cruel

The exiled Pandavas were roaming the forests. Lord Krishna happened to be with them. On the way, they came across an emaciated nomad and Bhima asked Krishna why God was so cruel that he had let that poor fellow become so weak. Krishna chose not to answer.

It was time to cook lunch and Bhima set out to fetch some bricks to help build a fire. He arrived at the fringe of the forest and saw a magnificent palace and an old, dilapidated structure nearby. He decided not to deface the beauty of the palace and instead, struck a blow at the walls of the ruined structure and took out some bricks and returned.

Lunch and siesta over, Krishna asked Bhima, 'How did you get the bricks?' Bhima told him, and Krishna asked, 'Why did you choose to avoid the palace? For all your strength, you could have easily taken out the bricks from the walls of the palace'. Disgruntled, Bhima replied, 'Will it be prudent on my part to spoil the beauty of a solid building? A derelict structure is anyway of no use, so I chose it'.

Krishna said, 'Yes. The stronger survive while, the weaker get exploited. God is not cruel. He gives to all, the strength and opportunity to grow. Those who use and gain strength, not only on the physical level but also on the subtle mental levels, by adhering to values and traditions, can safeguard themselves against exploitation and dishonour. Those who allow their strength to rot and become weak get trampled upon by the strong.

Now Bhima had the answer to his question.

The above episode involving Lord Krishna and Bhima is interesting, Yogi. I have not heard this before. Okay, then what is the connection here to Korporate DNA?

CY: Let me share an interesting event from world history to leverage the points from the above episode that I want to connect to Korporate DNA. Do you recall a movie called *300*? It is a movie based on events during a historical war, known as the Battle of Thermopylae, between Persia and Greece in 480 BCE. The massive Persian army was led by King Xerxes and the comparatively smaller Greek army (an alliance of Greek city-states) by King Leonidas of the state of Sparta. The vastly outnumbered Greek army fought valiantly against the massive legions of the Persians for several days, before getting annihilated in the end. Despite losing their men, the warriors of the Greek army fought to their last breath and their heroic efforts to save the larger interests of their land and their tradition and culture remain etched in the history of Greece. They lost the war but won the hearts of their countrymen.

The similarity between the Pandavas who fought the Mahabharata war and the Greeks, lies in the collective spirit of unity that both exhibited to establish the cherished values of their land.

Would you term the collective values displayed by them (Pandavas/ Spartans/Greeks) as their 'Korporate DNA'?

CY: Let me rephrase it. How often do you find CEOs investing time in building a combined value system or the Korporate DNA for their organisation? In their exaggerated focus on financials, they tend to overlook the fact that cherished values and principles contribute to laying a firm and solid foundation for organisations to stand tall and strong, and speak for themselves, defying time-tested factors. It is true that some organisations do develop a set of lofty values and ethics, but, somewhere along the way, they buckle under pressure and deviate from the path; it is mandatory that any individual or organisation steadfastly live by their proclaimed values, lest the values get side-lined and over a period of time, are relegated to mere posters on the wall.

A Spiritual CEO would be more inclined towards building a team of winners by infusing high values and an element of cultural identity, which would eventually translate into, and reflect as, positive responses in everyday activities.

How often do you find organisations identifying and reminiscing the contributions of significant and influential figures from the organisation's past and inculcating their admirable spirit and values into those currently being recruited? Imagine a scenario where recruits, on their first day at work, are introduced to the colourful history and tradition of the organisation, and to all those whose singular purpose was the welfare and growth of the organisation *they* now work for. Imagine the galvanising effect this could have on the freshers.

Just as we are impressed by the victory of good over evil in the Mahabharata war, and just as we are awestruck by watching the movie *300,* depicting the heroism of the Spartans, motivational exercises and activities explained above, will put the team members in a broader context of identifying themselves as part of the rich history of the organisation, instead of being merely a part of the workforce. Every organisation will have a history and tradition from which its founders derived their pride in success and achievement, and anyone working for the organisation ought to carry their own share of pride by contributing to the success of the organisation.

What would be the takeaways for a CEO from the two impressive episodes given above?

CY: You can shortlist some lessons from the following, though there can be a wide range of possibilities apart from what I am giving you here:

Lesson 1: The CEO needs to be a powerful and effective leader.

Lesson 2: Impart values and ethics to the employees and foster a work culture that promotes loyalty and strict adherence to core values.

Lesson 3: Courage has an intrinsic value.

Lesson 4: Virtues in life can prove to be worthier than life itself.

Lesson 5: Integrity has a priority over everything else, no matter what the circumstance or how much one has to lose.

Lesson 6: Always put your people first.

Lesson 7: A CEO must be ready to make sacrifices, if the situation requires it.

Lesson 8: Keep empowering.

How would all this impact the bottom line of the organisation?

CY: Let me share one of my favourite quotes in this regard.

> *I will tell His Majesty what a king is. A king does not abide within his tent while his men bleed and die upon the field. A king does not dine while his men go hungry, nor sleep when they stand at watch upon the wall. A king does not command his men's loyalty through fear nor purchase it with gold; he earns their love by the sweat of his own back and the pains he endures for their sake. That which comprises the harshest burden, a king lifts first and sets down last. A king does not require the service of those he*

leads but provides it to them. He serves them, not they him'. (From *Gates of Fire* by Steven Pressfield).

As Yogi went into a thoughtful mood, I gently nudged him, 'My question is waiting for an answer.'

CY: Let us see what the Spartans in the movie *300* and Yudhishthira, the paragon of virtue in the Mahabharata, stood for at critical junctures. When it came to the Spartans, the situation demanded very brave and daring decisions, which many leaders would have backed away from taking. With Yudhishthira, he had to fight his own brothers and the acharyas, stronger and mightier than his army, yet he didn't buckle in spite of severe setbacks on every day of the war.

They were faced with decisions that most leaders would comfortably back away from taking. Not them. Undaunted and fearless, they trespassed into no-man's land to save their land and people.

Many of the qualities and virtues we talked about in this section have been essential across all periods of time, and in today's corporate world, they are all the more important and indispensable as the high values of the past are getting corroded and employees' loyalty and integrity is at an all-time low. Unsurprising, considering employees are merely used as pawns in the game of getting a better-shaped P&L (Profit and Loss account) and B/S (Balance Sheet). These qualities are so important that when the chips are on the table, people know where you stand and know that you won't falter or be coerced into bad choices. So many decisions made in boardrooms across the world don't put people first. They are more concerned with the bottom line and how their (CEOs) personal bonuses are affected. Now, I'm no fool. I do understand that companies are in business to make money. And the perennial question remains—what came first, chicken or the egg? History has shown that you can cut costs and maintain jobs. Sure, there is sacrifice, but in the short term. It is in the long haul that it works out and all those involved come out ahead.

There are times when a CEO (as in the case of King Leonidas) knows that a lot of sacrifices are being made. But they are always for a larger good, as was proved for the Greeks when they won the war. When you as the CEO, and your team stand as testimonials for that kind of loyalty, values and beliefs, you will be greatly admired and respected and your ways emulated across the organisation. Sometimes as a CEO, to borrow from military terminology, you need to stand up front and take the bullet.... When you do all these, your people feel energised and truly empowered. It cannot be denied that sometimes you will have to pay the price for it in the short term, but the overall positive message you will send to your people and your superiors will be that you do not hesitate to go the extra mile, regardless of the cost.

And, believe me, it pays huge dividends (on all fronts) in the long run. After all, that is what genuine leadership is all about.

May we move to the rapid-fire Q&A round, Yogi?
CY: I am ready for that!

Rapid-fire Q&A on 'The Korporate DNA—A Place for Shared Traditions, Values and Beliefs'

How do I go about baselining what my company's current DNA is?
Let us understand what we are seeking before we find out how to seek it! Korporate DNA can be taken as a metaphor for the 'visions, values, and sense of purpose that bind an organisation together' to enable individuals to 'understand and absorb the mission and challenge of the whole enterprise'. The term Korporate DNA is sometimes used as shorthand for an organisation's culture and strategy—a metaphor for what makes it unique. It can also be seen as a way to understand the underlying organisational and cultural design factors that define an organisation's personality and determine whether it is strong or weak in executing strategy. Fortunately, there are several ways and methods that can be used to profile the DNA of your organisation. The HR team of your

organisation can work with specialists in this field who work on organisational DNA profiling. Using a framework that examines all aspects of a company's architecture, resources, and relationships, the tool allows management to gain insight into what is and is not working, deep inside a highly complex organisation.

My company's vision is primarily driven by customer delight and the bottom line. How can I bring a spiritual point of view into my new vision statement?
The vision you have outlined here are lag indicators (output/results), whereas organisational DNA is more of a lead indicator. Hence, bringing in a spiritual point of view into the lead indicators or your vision/mission statements should not be an issue. DNA gives the 'how' picture to the organisational stakeholders, primarily the employees.

Our value statements have become 'wall hangings'. How can I ingrain them deep into my company's culture and ethos?
You are right. Many years ago, when I walked into an organisation and found the quality statement on the desk of the receptionist, I asked her what it stood for. She said, 'I don't know; but I keep it here because it was developed by a team of experts and I was told to display it!' More than having them adorn the walls, the only way is for the CEO and top leaders to 'walk the talk' when it comes to their organisation's vision statement. Rather, be the value that you want your team to imbibe and follow. Please bear in mind: '*People don't do as you tell them to do, but they do as you do*'.

How do I leverage the strength of employee diversity for the benefit of my company's success?
As a CEO or as a leader, there are lots of things you can do to build and leverage such diversity. Unity of purpose amidst the diversity of the workforce is the key defining factor. Some of the steps you can consider implementing to nurture and leverage diversity are:

- Hire for diverse strengths, skills and experience.
- Help people appreciate the value of their own and others' strengths.

- Use character strengths, as well as skills, to allocate projects and tasks.
- Have frequent one-on-one conversations about strengths.
- Never neglect your workers.
- Encourage informal social activities.
- Challenge people to use their strengths in new and different ways.
- Focus on the strengths everybody brings to the table.
- Don't allow discrimination on any ground.
- Empower employees to utilise their strengths.
- Offer strong mentoring.

We started small but have grown through acquisitions. Any suggestions on how we can build a strong system of beliefs that permeates to all employees—regardless of which acquisition they came from?

M&As (mergers and acquisitions) are ticking time bombs on the DNA front. One research says, '83 per cent of all mergers and acquisitions failed to produce any benefit for the shareholders and over half actually destroyed value' (Study by Martin Roll Company). Interviews with over a hundred senior executives involved in these deals over two years revealed that the overwhelming cause for failure was 'the people and the cultural differences'. Hence, your question assumes great significance. Let me share a few insights on how you can look at building a value-based system to accommodate cultural diversity.

- *Accept and Adapt:* Form small, agile, quick-acting teams, including people from both sides of the M&As, with a clear mission, and empowered integration team managers, who have direct access to senior management and their support. Transitions do not need to be demonstrations of democracy in action.
- *Acceleration:* Speed up the integration to reduce uncertainty and anxiety.

- *Concentration:* During the first 90 days, focus on and get everyone to focus on 20 per cent of the goals that yield 80 per cent of the economic value.

The human and cultural issues that separate the 17 per cent from the 83 per cent are about the concrete reality of productivity, economic value and sustained growth.

How do I build elements of the Korporate DNA into the performance measurement of employees?

It is like opening a lock that needs multiple keys and one size doesn't fit all. Suffice to say that, as part of their goal sheets (or whatever performance measures you bring in), each employee must have behaviours that they must display (lead indicators) which, in turn, would help them demonstrate Korporate DNA. Sufficient focus must also be given to L&D (learning and development) to foster continuous inputs and improvements on this front.

I am looking at rearchitecting my organisation. Any guidance principles I ought to use to ensure that individual teams place emphasis on values and beliefs?

Whatever you want to do with your organisation or with your teams, please bear in mind that the entire purpose is to 'attract and retain the right talent'. A typical reorganisation takes ten months from plan to practice; you need to execute it well so as not to lose out on the benefits that can accrue for your organisation in the longer run. There is a statistic according to which 'only 23 per cent get it right'. Hence, the need to be extra vigilant in this process! You can keep the following principles in mind while redrawing your organisation:

Think beyond lines and boxes: The probability of success is low if companies address only structural elements, such as the lines and boxes of the organisational chart, roles and responsibilities, functions or businesses, insourcing or outsourcing, and governance. Process elements, such as standardisation, decision rights, performance management, and information flows are the second category to consider. The people elements of a redesign, including the size of the workforce, its skills, talent in general, and culture, must also be considered.

All three elements (structures, processes, and people) influence the way work gets done in companies, hence all three have to be balanced.

To build values, you can look at output or Lag Values (happiness, self-respect, family security, freedom, inner peace and harmony, and professional excellence, etc.) and Lead Values (honesty, sincerity, ambition, independence, obedience, courageousness, and competitiveness, etc.).

When we began, we had a bottom line focussed culture, which served initial growth. But over time, I am losing my key talent to burn out and other soft challenges. How do I bring compassionate and spiritual DNA into the company?

Companies that embed spiritual values and compassion in their businesses generate better financial performance, experience higher levels of employee retention and are able to drive customer loyalty, because employees and clients give back when they feel cared for and valued. Companies can have the most compelling vision and the clearest strategy, but if the culture is not conducive, compassion and spiritual values will never flourish. The origin of the word (compassion) is from the Latin for 'co-suffering'. A more modern definition from the Cambridge English Dictionary describes it as a 'strong feeling of sympathy and sadness for the suffering or bad luck of others and a wish to help them'. Organisations 'feel' the pain of their employees and stakeholders, but the question is, how many are ready to bite the bullet and do something about it? There is no one prescription or a magic formula that creates compassionate organisations. There are some indicators though, that helps build one. The key to this learning is that it takes time, it takes effort, and it can be hugely frustrating for leaders and employees alike. Some of the following inputs might help you build an organisation that helps spiritual and compassionate values to thrive:

- Employee-first decision-making: Rather than focussing on bottom-line-based decision-making it is best for organisation to focus on employees.
- Systems and practices: It is the policies and procedures that enshrine culture and help embed spiritual values and compassion in organisations.
- Building trust and respect: Research has shown that work practices founded upon trust and respect, such as transparent communication, participative decision-making, and favourable HR policies, are conducive to a spiritual and compassionate culture.

How would spiritually inclined leaders move away from micro-management to mature leadership?

A spiritual leader is someone who incorporates their beliefs into all matters of life. When our beliefs about the world inform our work, we lead more wholesome lives—lives that are truly more successful—than those who don't integrate their beliefs with the rest of their life. Since spiritual values teach you to 'let go', you don't worry about checking with your team every now and then to see how things are going. Such enlightened leaders trust their employees more and don't breathe down their necks from close quarters, which micro-managers tend to do. They are high on motivation and empowerment and hence don't feel the need for stepping in time and again. They give lots of space for innovation and hence employee engagement is quite high, thereby reducing the need for micro-managing. Spiritual leaders are those who move from external power and control to internal/inner balance and harmony. There are several concepts, frameworks, tools and techniques (shared throughout this book) to achieve this. You can pick a few to start with and then gradually build on them as you progress.

Can you paint the picture of an ideal organisation that is well-oiled in terms of recognising and measuring its Korporate DNA?

You will find several or almost all of the following eleven qualities in organisations where Korporate DNA is well defined:

1. Purpose (direction orientation)
2. Priority (value orientation)
3. Community (people orientation)
4. Values (fairness orientation)
5. Innovation (risk orientation)
6. Attention to detail (precision orientation)
7. Emphasis on processes (effort orientation)
8. Emphasis on outcome (achievement orientation)
9. Teamwork (collaboration orientation)
10. Aggressiveness (competitive orientation)
11. Stability (rule orientation)

Looking Glass—The Korporate DNA—A Place for Shared Traditions, Values and Beliefs

Key Takeaways:

» Korporate DNA can be taken as a metaphor for the 'visions, values, and a sense of purpose that bind an organisation together'.

» The combined values of a team, however small or outnumbered they may be, are far superior to an incoherent (on values) large team in the final outcome.

» Leaders have to demonstrate genuineness—by leading from the front, demonstrating courage and making sacrifices.

» Mergers and acquisitions are a ticking time bomb on the DNA front. Hence, care has to be exercised, so core values aren't eroded.

» Leaders have to become walking ambassadors of their company DNA and value statements.

Action Points:

» Design or enhance your company DNA over the next 90-days.

» Recognize and reward those championing diversities in your organisation.
» Create a storyboard from the traditions and history of your company which can be used as inputs for values.
» Set up measurement criteria to check on alignment with company's values, especially for managers.
» Reflect on two or three instances where you could have done a better job as CEO to demonstrate genuine leadership.

6

Who is a Spiritual CEO? The Conundrum of Body, Mind and Soul Being in Balance

asaktabuddhihi sarvatra jitaatmaa vigatasprihaa |
naishkarmyasiddhim paramaam sanyaasenaadhigachhati ||

One whose mind is unattached from all aspects, who is self-controlled, from whom desires have departed, attains the supreme state of freedom from action by sanyaasa

|| Gita: Ch. 18 – v. 49 ||

Heaven Bound ...

It was time for the Pandava brothers to renounce their kingdom, transfer power to the next in line and begin their final journey to heaven. All five brothers, along with Draupadi, set out to ascend to heaven on Mount Sumeru. On the way, a dog struck a wonderful camaraderie with them and joined them in their journey.

En route, Draupadi and four of the brothers met with their end. They were bound to earth by their various attachments (arising out of body-mind-sense complexities) and Yudhishthira alone made it alive. Yudhishthira, the icon of dharma, as his name itself indicates (Yudhi + Sthira = one who remains steadfast in the battle between dharma and adharma), was in control of the whole spectrum of mental states and liberation was beckoning him.

What kind of bondages could have contributed to the journey getting aborted midway for the others?

Draupadi:	Predilection for Arjuna.
Sahadeva:	Though virtuous and exemplary in character, the vanity and pride in his own wisdom.
Nakula:	Obsession with his physical looks and associated pride.
Arjuna:	Immense pride in his skill as the most powerful warrior in the world.
Bhima:	Insatiable appetite for food.

As Yudhishthira and the dog continued their journey, Indra appeared with his chariot and offered to take Yudhishthira to heaven. Yudhishthira wanted to take the dog with him, which Indra refused. Yudhishthira was not willing to betray his companion for his own comfort. Seeing his unwavering stance, the dog transformed into the god of Dharma and they both entered the gates of heaven.

Yogi, may I know the connection between this incident in the Mahabharata and a Spiritual CEO?

CY: In the previous five chapters, we studied the many-faceted aspects of the Spiritual CEO's role in the organisation. There is one important fundamental point that we cannot afford to ignore. A Biblical quote comes to my mind: 'For what profits a man if he gains the whole world but loses his own soul'. Likewise, what good will come out of it, if the organisation flourishes but the CEO himself loses his soul? While many CEOs are working tirelessly promoting and furthering the financial prospects of their respective organisations, and in the process, setting an example for others too: Are they taking care of themselves?

Can you provide a deeper insight into this, Yogi?

The body, mind and soul should all be aligned and congruent with our identity and how we present ourselves to the world. While people tend to think they understand the body aspects (I have my doubts about their level of understanding) and mind aspects to a great extent, when it comes to an understanding the 'soul', people are not so sure of their level of understanding. The soul forms the core of our existence and we need to ensure we have a harmonious and integrated relationship among the three—body, mind and soul. The absence of a rapport among the three coordinates, which is pivotal to how our personalities shape up, would result in our moving around like zombies, attending to every beck and call of the board, the market, the clientele and forgetting to really 'live' for ourselves.

Working towards bettering the financial results of the organisation and remaining smugly content with providing himself/herself a luxurious lifestyle are not the only milestones in life that a CEO should be chasing. The need for an objective, or rather I would call it, a philosophy, to bring about a drastic change at the root level has been recognised and is getting promulgated and popularised: it is not just work-life balance anymore but work-life harmony that is gaining momentum.

Creating harmony between one's work and personal life will translate into a healthy outlook towards both aspects of living, and a rhythm that instils a sense of belonging and fulfilment to one's existence itself, will fall into place unobtrusively. By identifying ourselves with whatever purpose we may be involved in, and being alive to the present moment of action, we can bring all the vital coordinates into a harmonious state of fusion, as it was in the case of Yudhishthira.

As a CEO, you have the privilege to exert great influence around you. So, you should aim at being an inspiration to not just a few, but the maximum number of people, to bring about a state of harmony in their work and lives, by setting the example of yourself being a picture of harmony and stability.

You said you have your own doubts regarding peoples' understanding of the body. Can you explain?

CY: We don't just stop with the idea of being 'body beautiful', but we probe further into the nutritional values of our food intake and try to create awareness about what types of food provide the necessary nourishment for a healthy body and proper functioning of the vital organs. This kind of physiological awareness is all about the derivatives from the various foods we partake—the calories, carbs, proteins, minerals, vitamins etc.

But there is another kind of much deeper study, a concept in yogic science known as the 'three gunas', which is said to be the basis of and provides the structure to human character traits and behavioural patterns. The three gunas are Rajas, Tamas and Sattva. And which of the three gunas plays a prominent role in an individual's personality and development is directly related to the nature of food that the individual partakes regularly. So, the essence of the concept is the nature of food that one consumes has a regulatory impact on how one develops and presents himself/herself as a human being.

Let me enumerate the characteristic qualities of these three gunas and then connect back to how the food habits of humans have a direct bearing on the body, the mind and the soul.

Rajasic qualities are: zealous activity, restlessness, stress and anger.

Tamasic qualities are: lethargy, ignorance, grossness and laziness.

Sattvic qualities are: balance, harmony, purity, health and well-being.

A Rajasic diet: Food items that are rich in sugar, oil, spices, onion and garlic, that contain taste enhancers, chocolate varieties, hot drinks like coffee and tea, carbonated drinks, etc.—all this form a diet of Rajasic nature. These foods may give an instant energy boost, but ultimately, they will leave the person hyperactive and with increased stress. A diet that predominately contains the above items will destroy the mind-body equilibrium, feeding the body at the expense of the mind. A Rajasic person will grab something on the run and eat in a rush, and as a result, will begin to suffer from poor digestion and associated health issues.

A Tamasic diet: Food items consisting of animal protein, such as meat, fish, poultry and eggs, stale and reheated foods, processed and canned foods containing chemical additives, takeaway fast food, junk food, and addiction-causing substances like tobacco, alcohol, drugs, etc. form a diet of Tamasic nature. Sattvic food can degenerate into Tamasic food when it is processed or fried or leftover item. A diet predominantly consisting of the above items and substances will do nothing to lift our energy and consciousness; instead, it will pull us downward into laziness and inertia and turn us into unmotivated, careless and dull-witted individuals. In the long run, such indiscriminate eating will lead to health complications such as obesity, diabetes, heart and liver disease and so on.

A Sattvic diet: Fresh fruit and vegetables, fruit and vegetable juices, whole-wheat bread, pulses, grains and sprouts, nuts, seeds, honey, herbs, milk and other dairy products which are free of animal rennet, natural foods, etc.—all this form a diet of Sattvic nature. These foods provide the ideal nourishment for the human system as a whole; they help raise our consciousness, unleash our hidden potential, energise, rejuvenate and motivate us to engage in positive and productive activities, and inspire us to follow meditation and other refinement practices. Sattvic food gets cooked with love and eaten with full awareness and gratitude.

So, now you can understand that the aspect of body awareness does not stop with external beauty and maintenance. It goes deep down into the very fundamental structure of an individual's distinctive and unique personality.

Can you explain how food habits affect the other two aspects of a human being, the mind and the soul?

CY: A person whose food habits fall in any one of the above categories will, by nature, adopt and reflect the qualities of the corresponding guna. Whichever guna is predominantly exercising its sway over us, will have a direct influence on our behaviour, attitude, actions, attachments and on how we perceive the world around us. For example, a person who is predominant in Tamas will see everything as negative and destructive. On the other hand, a person who is more Sattvic will find joy and happiness in everything. However, the mind is very unstable and fluid and can fluctuate very easily from one predominant guna to another. The functioning of the mind has its roots in the food intake and to create a fine balance of mind, body and soul, a person of viveka (one who can discriminate) knows how to balance his food intake so that he is able to maintain a balanced mix of all three diet patterns: Rajas (for that zeal and action), Tamas (for the character needed to survive in this materially-and-financially-focussed world) and Satvik (for that harmony on all fronts).

So, the bottom line is, a balanced diet will make a person more spiritual?

CY: More than my words, next time you eat something, check which category (Rajas, Tamas or Sattvic) the particular food item belongs to and observe how it affects your thought process and moods. When you notice a difference, it will be an opportunity for you to regulate or embrace your mental state, based on the nature of your observations. Precisely for this reason, yoga (all eight steps of Ashtanga Yoga and not just the asanas and pranayama alone) took centrestage in the ancient lifestyle in India: Yama and Niyama (the first two steps of Ashtanga Yoga) shared the life values (control and rules of personal conduct), Asanas and Pranayama (for a healthy and pure body), Prathyahara and Dharana (ability to withdraw into oneself and observe anything of one's choice through concentration), Dhyana and Samadhi (ability to meditate or go within into a state of enquiry and find complete equilibrium or balance through the process of Samadhi). It all starts with the first step of Yama and when you fail there, each one of the subsequent seven steps gets heavily compromised. To cap it all, it boils down to what types of food we consume essentially, and hence the balance (or equilibrium) of body, mind and soul starts with one's physical self, which consists of the inside and outside (of the body).

Would it be alright if I say that food and exercise are like lead indicators for the efficiency of the body, which is the Lag Indicator?
CY: Spot on. I am impressed. You can't expect to score 100 per cent in your mathematics examination if you don't attend classes and clock the hours at practising the learning through sums and homework.

So, how does one make these choices?
CY: Do you recall the conversation we had about 'viveka'? Viveka lets you discriminate and make choices. You can keep 'cause' or 'effect' as your input choice and, invariably, all actions arising out of such choices will lead to consequences. Even if someone thinks I am insane to spend so much time explaining about food, I am only putting forth the choices you have, based on 'cause' and 'effect'. The 'free will' option is very much there and one must take complete accountability for one's choice and its output thereof. Of course, when in doubt, you can listen to knowledgeable people who can offer you neutral, unbiased, down-to-earth, straight-on-the-face inputs without the need to sugar-coat their words. If, at the level of a CEO, one still needs things to be sugar-coated, then one is seriously handicapped in realising their true inner potential.

One of the prerequisites to be able to make the right choices is a stable and silent mind—in addition to awareness itself. So, techniques such as meditation help us remain grounded and make choices in a mental atmosphere of confidence and serenity.

What about the soul? How are the three elements of body, mind and soul connected to each other? How does their connectedness impact our lives?

CY: Our body, mind (including our emotions) and soul may seem to be separate elements independent of each other, but they are intimately connected and interdependent. When they are harmoniously integrated, they make the unique human existence complete in all aspects. The thread of connectivity that runs through our body, mind and soul keeps sharing and echoing their experiences, so, what we experience in one particular element, will get transmitted to the other elements too. For instance, when we experience disease or pain in our body, our mind and soul also get affected. When negative thoughts or fear occur in our mind, the body tenses up and triggers the nervous responses; likewise, the soul gets subtly impacted by the formation of negative energy or negative karma.

When we experience negative emotions like sorrow, anger or disappointment, and when our connection to the inner core, the soul, is frail, we turn to our mind and body to find answers to our mood upheavals. The soul is the mute witness to what goes on in the other two areas, the body and the mind. When we work towards 'integration' of body, mind and soul, we are tracing our way back to the original, natural harmony that always existed.

As humans, we tend to focus on symptoms and search for alleviation through another symptom. For example, when we have body pain or we are under emotional turmoil, we seek remedy through another symptom like alcohol.

The root cause lies in the imbalance and disharmony we have created among these three elements, which affects us and affects the environment around us … this holds true for an organisation and its CEO as well.

What is the soul's true calling?

CY: For this, you must find the higher purpose of your life. What is your soul's calling? What are the personal values you will stand up for, at any cost? What is the true inner search that will keep you in perfect harmony under all circumstances? 'The happiest man is he who is happy under all circumstances', said a great saint of India, known as Babuji Maharaj of Shahjahanpur, Uttar Pradesh. Very wise words indeed!

A soul's true calling is best understood by each individual on their own! Copying a template from someone else's life might not be best suited for you. Having said that, there are several examples and stories out there, from time immemorial, which will tell you that a man remains unhappy till such time that he has found his soul's calling. Whatever it might be, if man is ready to silence his mind and listen to his heart, he will find the answer. The day he finds it, the search ends and a new search begins. In simple terms, you might call it the 'true meaning of life or the soul's calling' and it could be anything; your family, your society, your existence, God or the Supreme Power or whatever. You need to find it; and the body and mind are the only means bestowed upon you to help in the search; and there lies the primary reason for the need to keep them in balance, lest you lose focus on the way.

Time for a rapid-fire Q&A round, Yogi?
CY: Sure.

Rapid-fire Q&A on 'Who is a Spiritual CEO? The Conundrum of Body, Mind and Soul Being in Balance'

I hear a lot of talk on 'spirituality in management' etc. Can you share a few perspectives on this?
Spiritual leadership involves the application of spiritual values and principles to the workplace. The spiritual leader understands the importance of employees finding fulfilment and meaning in their work, and demonstrates a genuine concern for the 'whole' person, not just the employee. Please bear in mind that not all spirituality is religious, but all religions espouse a distinctive spirituality. Modern-

day leaders are ready to accept, as minimum standard, the following as the definition for spirituality: 'The feelings, thoughts, experiences, and behaviours that arise from a search for the sacred.' The concept of 'servant leadership' (a sub set of Spiritual Leadership) which is widely accepted and practised these days comes from the spiritual leanings of a leader. Spiritual leadership is viewed as an effective way to fuel employees' intrinsic motivation. Spiritual leadership not only caters to the psychological needs of both leaders and followers but also taps into the fundamental needs for spiritual survival, which include spiritual values and management practices, such as inspiring people to seek interesting and meaningful work. The purpose of spiritual leadership is to intrinsically motivate followers by means of practicing spiritual values and exhibiting altruistic love in the workplace. Followers of leaders with spiritual leanings are more likely to perform better because of a common and clear vision.

Spiritual leadership can be a balanced combination of working towards a) vision and performance, b) instilling hope and faith, and c) creation of an altruistic love for and among all employees. Ethics, morality and benevolence, all will find a place in the spiritual leadership canvas too.

A CEO's role is a high-pressure job with limited time to spare. How do I find time for spiritual pursuits?

If you have to cut a tree you need to spend a fair amount of time sharpening the axe. The same is true for a high-performing CEO facing a high-pressure job. When you touch their minds, people are willing to walk a dozen miles for you; and when you touch their hearts, people are willing to walk a thousand miles for you; but when you touch their souls, people are willing to walk a million miles for you. And each of these three steps (touching the minds, hearts and souls) has its own ROI. It is up to you to decide which makes sense. I am not selling the concept of financial ROI but ROI of a different paradigm. Think about it.

There is a Zen quote: 'You should sit in meditation for twenty minutes a day. Unless you're too busy, then you should sit for an hour'. This saying gets to the heart of what is important in life. So, if one understands the soft ROI of it—one will make the time.

Can a CEO truly be tough and spiritual at the same time? Sounds like they don't go together!

In the Indian context, there is the analogy of a jackfruit: very rough and tough on the outside but the fruit inside is so sweet and delicious. A spiritual leader has to be like that. He looks tough to the world or even to his team members, but inside he is a man of substance and high empathy. Those around him might take time to get used to this but they all know that 'he is there for them'. It is a paradox but something worth understanding and growing into.

I am already doing basic walking and jogging in my daily routine. As a CEO should I be doing more? Does yoga play a role?

I think we dealt with this in a detailed manner when we talked about the balance of body, mind and soul in this very chapter. It is important to take a holistic approach to your daily living. When we are focussed only on our physical frame, activities you described may look sufficient—but certainly not when we look at the full picture.

Being strong in mind is a prerequisite for me and my leadership—it enables me to make tough and important decisions. How can I inculcate such values, thoughts and working ethos into my team culture?

It is like the question of what came first: the chicken or the egg. Values come first and within that framework decisions are to be made. Tough and hard decisions are not necessarily negative in nature. When the values include mutual trust and respect for all your employees and team members, they will come forward to help you while making tough choices and decisions. Just to help you understand this, let me explain what trust and respect are. Trust can be defined as 'When everyone involved fully and firmly believes that his/her interest is fully protected in the decision that has been taken' and respect can be defined as: 'When I can express my views to anyone in the organisation, albeit politely, without having to worry about protecting my back later!' If such trust and respect exists, everything else will follow.

The concept of the CEO focussing on the soul sounds esoteric. Is there ROI for a CEO to take a 'soulful' approach to leadership?
Do you recall the story of the Pandavas and the Spartans? There is a famous quote: 'People don't care how much you know till they know how much you care'. When they have a leader who lives by certain values, in which they feel wanted, respected, valued and cared for, the entire force will be behind such a leader. However smart a CEO may be, he still needs his entire team to put their weight behind him, in full. It is not his individual performance, hence, that matters but his ability to synergise his entire team and stay unitedly focussed on the organisation's goals. What better options are there than to lead them with a set of 'spiritual values'?

These days I keep hearing of overall well-being. What does this mean for my corporate workforce?
It means the same as what it means to a CEO. Keeping body, mind and soul in balance and harmony; a well-nourished and well-balanced individual, inside out, is a far better asset to himself and to the organisation in the longer run.

The body, mind and soul sound like three disparate items. Is there really a connection between them in a corporate context?
Do you recall the example of the executive (Chapter 4—Hub and Spoke)? Man, by nature, must be multifaceted in his life in order for him to get the best. A well-nourished and rested body, mind and soul is necessary for the person to perform at his peak, in a sustained way. If you look at athletes, you will find them quickly resting in bursts (even when the sporting event is going on); else they will collapse. It is a structural issue. Once you construct a

building do you leave it at that, or do you have periodical stress tests to check how the building is standing up?

A corporate organisation is nothing but a large collection of individuals who are driven by a common set of values and a well-defined purpose. If individuals get balanced in the three dimensions, it follows that the teams and the organisation, as a whole, benefit.

How can a Spiritual CEO mitigate risks?

He puts in Korporate DNA or values in place; he creates a sustainable workplace. He adds on top the layers of 'spiritual workplace' (maintaining positive employee attitudes and behaviours), and 'spiritual leadership' qualities. Spiritual leaders, by their sustained practice, also build a level of intuition which normally eludes those who are focussed on performance only. They meditate very often, they know how to look outside and look within, they know how to calm their mind and look for potential pitfalls in the future. Of course, they have a well-oiled team in place, which adds the necessary support layers. In a sublime way, the Spiritual CEO learns and adapts to anticipate and proactively mitigate most risks before they emerge. Their inner radars become very well-tuned and fine instruments, while externally they remain as sharp as ever.

How do I measure if I or my leader has indeed embraced a spiritual approach to our leadership?

There are a few qualities that spiritually-aligned leaders exhibit. You might want to check if you tick a few or all of these boxes:

- They lead others to discover their own purpose and identity.
- They lead others into transformation—not just production.
- They impact the surrounding atmosphere.
- They help people see old things in new ways.
- They gain a following because of who they are—not because of the position they hold.
- They are of proven character.

- They remain humble, well-grounded and have a genuine love for people.

I could add more to this list, but this should suffice for starters.

Looking Glass—**Who is a Spiritual CEO? The Conundrum of Body, Mind and Soul Being in Balance.**

Key Takeaways:

» For a CEO's overall well-being, the alignment of body, mind and soul is important.
» Food intake has an impact on our mind and soul, as well as our body.
» Developing a sharpened level of discrimination (*vairagya*) helps in making good choices.
» Everyone, especially a CEO, has to introspect to determine and answer his true calling.
» A good spiritual leader understands the importance of employees finding meaning in their work and demonstrates a genuine concern for the 'whole' person.

Action Points:

» Organise a workshop for employees to help them discover their true calling in the context of your company's corporate values.
» Engage experts who can raise awareness about the types of foods and their impact on body, mind and soul.
» Setup a yoga awareness workshop where employees can learn about all the aspects of Ashtanga Yoga.
» Develop a programme to incorporate meditation into the corporate life of employees.
» Request HR to ensure there is space in the office (or create it) where employees can engage in well-being activities during office breaks.

7

Past, Erase and Go

shreyo hi jñanam abhyasaj jñanad dhyanarh vishishyate
dhyanat karma-phala-tyagas tyaga chchhantir anantaram | |

Better than mechanical practice is knowledge; better than knowledge is meditation; even better than meditation is abandonment of the fruits of action. For such abandonment, is immediately followed by peace.

| | Gita Ch.12-V.12 | |

The King Who Become a Brahma Rishi ...

Sage Vishwamitra was a Kshatriya by birth. He was a valiant king by the name of Kaushika who ruled the kingdom of Kadhi. A bizarre turn of events led Kaushika to relinquish his kingship and engage in intense penance and come to be known as Brahmarishi Vishwamitra.

The prelude to the change in the king's life was his courtesy visit to the hermitage of the great sage Vasishtha. The sage entertained the king and his entourage to a sumptuous feast. Kaushika was surprised that a sage living in a hermitage could serve such a grand feast to so many people. Vasishtha told him about Nandini, the calf of the celestial cow Kamadhenu, and said she was a gift from God Indra and she would give him anything he wished for. Kaushika wanted to take the calf with him and when Vasishtha refused, a war ensued and Vasishtha, through his Brahmashakti powers, defeated Kaushika and his large army.

Kaushika, despite facing defeat, was highly impressed by the efficacy and greatness of yogic power and renouncing his kingdom, began his quest to become like Vasishtha, through intense penance. As he began to acquire extraordinary yogic powers, he began to preen himself on his achievements and Indra found him an impending threat to the celestial gods. So, Indra sent Menaka, a beautiful celestial nymph, to lure Kaushika and nullify his yogic powers. She succeeded and they lived together. In the course of time, Kaushika came to know of the dubious intentions of Menaka, cursed her and retreated to the Himalayas to undertake strenuous forms of penance to annihilate his weaknesses. His arduous penance finally culminated in the realisation of his alchemical dream. Lord Brahma bestowed upon Kaushika the honourable title 'Brahmarishi' and gave him the name Sage Vishwamitra.

Sage Vishwamitra went to meet Vasishtha. The custom was for the lesser sage to greet the superior one and, in turn, receive the superior's blessings; and in case of equal status, both sages would greet each other. Vishwamitra greeted Vasishtha with the pride of being a Brahmarishi, but Vasishtha simply blessed him, thus treating him as the lesser. Vishwamitra realised his mistake and felt humbled and Vasishtha instinctively saw the transformation in Vishwamitra, acknowledged the equality between them and greeted Vishwamitra. The enmity among them ended and they united in the sanctity of their yogic powers.

Dear Yogi, that is a nice story. Would you like to expand on what you want to communicate through this story?

CY: In a way, we are all like Vishwamitra in that we all have the inbuilt capacity to master change and thereby transform and metamorphose like he did. Many of us need external triggers to activate the change process. In the case of Vishwamitra, it came through Sage Vasishtha. Such triggers do present themselves in our lives too, but we tend to miss them, because the ego in us gets offended and bruised and instead of using the opportunity to our advantage, we get into fight or flight mode. Of course, not all insults and adversities produce such great opportunities for transformation, as was the case with Vishwamitra, but some do come our way and we have to identify them.

Let us look at it from another perspective. Vishwamitra's life, as a king, was rich and comfortable and was going on with clockwork precision or like a missile on its chartered course ... that is, until there was external interference. When he got upset at Vasishtha's refusal to part with his calf Nandini, and subsequently had to face defeat in the war, it generated a major change of mind in him; he allowed his discriminative intellect to guide him and chose to follow the path of 'Viveka'. Was that the effect or the cause? He could have chosen to resume the war with Vasishtha and could have even spent his entire lifetime repeatedly waging wars against the unconquerable Vasishtha, but instead he was prudent enough to alter the very course of his life. The missile can be made to alter its trajectory and move in a different direction by reprogramming the computer code on the missile.

How do you think a Spiritual CEO would adapt to the learning?

CY: You see, at every juncture in your life, you will be having two choices. One will be to 'react to the past' and the reaction will have a direct influence on your current thinking and subsequently unfold as current events in your life. The other choice will be to 'pause, analyse and learn from the past'. The analytical thinking will open up more possibilities in the current scheme of things, for you to choose to do, redo or undo.

If you have seen any time travel movies, that is precisely what they attempt to do. To change an event waiting to happen in the present, they travel back in time into the past, change a related event there and thus facilitate the current event to change correspondingly. It is of course a fantasy, for us to change the events in the past to bring about a different outcome to an impending event in the present. But, what we can surely do is to adopt a proactive approach instead of a reactive one, and turn out to be creative architects of a better and different future.

That is precisely what Vishwamithra did. He could have simply stationed himself in the reactive mode and ended up waging war after war against Vasishtha, but he didn't do it.

He was shrewd enough to realise that the key to making a breakthrough in the impasse, was not about acquiring possession of the celestial calf, but to aim to acquire similar special powers as the person who was in possession of the calf, in this case Sage Vasishtha. Instead of fighting for the Calf (effect or result), he turned his attention to the Power (cause or root) which was Vasishtha himself.

Once he was firmly set on his coveted goal of acquiring extraordinary yogic powers through practice of penance, his onboard computer program received the inputs and updated its executable. Despite facing several obstructive tactics and pitfalls, nothing could stop him (remember the butterfly metaphor?), from transforming and metamorphosing into a Brahmarishi, the Supreme honour that placed him at par with the august Sage Vasishtha, his once-upon-a-time tormentor-in-chief!

Viswamithra created a new world for himself, on his own terms, and quite literally one for Thrishanku, king of the Ishvaku dynasty, too. That is another popular Puranik story in which king Thrishanku, who tried to enter heaven in his mortal body, was denied entry there and had to remain suspended. Viswamithra, seeing his plight, created a world for him to reside in, midway between heaven and earth, known as Thrishanku Sorgam (paradise). It is also a pointer to Trishanku's indefatigable spirit, as he had to continue to go through several challenges and traumatic experiences for the rest of his life, but he learnt his lessons well.

What are the concrete steps a leader or a Spiritual CEO has to undertake in this undoing and redoing process?

CY: The key is to be fully immersed in the present. There is nothing more powerful and productive in the life of a human being than to be 'in the moment' or 'in the present'. It is the single point in time from where all activities encapsulated in the framework of past, present and future, generate and manifest. The present moment is where one can reminisce about the past to learn from mistakes, rectify or redo or undo them, and at the same time sow the seeds for creating a compelling future. So, the present moment is the only point in time alive, throbbing and vibrating, for man to activate all his faculties and embark on a well-thought out action plan that will help him to redesign his destiny.

At this point of time, I will share an interesting anecdote from the Mahabharata, which explains the need to act in the present moment, in a convincing manner.

It was a fine morning, and Yudhishtra was relaxing in the front yard of his house, when a beggar came asking for alms. Yudhishthira told him he was busy and asked him to come the next day, and the beggar went away. Bhima, who was watching all this, picked up a drum and started to run towards the people of the town, shouting excitedly. Yudhishtra stopped him and asked him what the matter was.

Bhima replied, 'I am going to inform the people that my brother has conquered time, because he has made a promise for tomorrow. Are you sure you or the beggar will be alive tomorrow? Do you know for sure that tomorrow you would be in a charitable mood and give alms to the beggar? Is it certain that tomorrow this beggar would remain a beggar? And are you sure that you and the beggar would see each other again tomorrow? It seems you have conquered time and I should tell Krishna and all the others about this great event; I have to hurry. I don't want to miss this hour because I will not get it back again'

Yudhishthira realised his imprudence and said to Bhima, 'Yes. I made a grave mistake. He alone can make such a promise who has attained 'supreme freedom'. Call the beggar back so I can give him something right now. Tomorrow is really unknown'.

Very interesting! Can you expand on the topic 'Present'?

CY: The secret of health for both mind and the body is not to mourn for the past, worry about the future, or anticipate troubles, but to live in the present moment wisely and earnestly.

While being in this topic, we need to know that there is a big difference between 'living for the moment' and 'living in the moment'. In 'living for the moment' there will be expectations and in 'living in the moment' there are absolutely none. In the words of Lord Krishna, 'living in the present or moment' is the essence of the life of a Karma Yogi. The powerful message here is to 'focus on the efforts and not on the results'. May not sound easy, but it is definitely doable!

If you take the example of stock markets, the best advice for investors is not to worry about the short-term market situations but to stay invested. Fluctuations will come and go but the slow upward gains of the market won't stop, at least not in the longer run. Millions of dollars being wiped off the market capitalisation value or millions being added to the same are part and parcel of financials. Not bothering about the results and instead putting your full potential in the efforts will help you to maintain the innermost harmony and equanimity too, since you are not weighed down by anticipation and anxiety. A simple explanation is enough to make you understand this; just look at Circle of Influence (COI) and Circle of Concern (COC). You can't change the weather (COC) but taking an umbrella is in your control (COI). You can't control others' reactions (COC) but you can surely moderate your temper or reactions (COI). That is the focus in Zen too—'Be in the moment'.

Children, by nature, stay focussed in the present; we can see children fighting seriously one moment and the next moment they would forget everything, become buddies again and continue to play with each other as if nothing happened; but it will be a different case with their parents; they will continue to be at loggerheads over whose child started the fight. The animals too, by default, stay focussed in the present. Observe a predator waiting to pounce on its prey; it directs its full focus on the present moment, no distractions, no wavering, gathers all its energy on the action of the moment and pounces on its prey. The same set of behaviours will be seen in the prey too as it tries to gather all its energy and focus on escape modes.

The emphasis on 'being in the moment' will be more pronounced in the field of sports and corporate work environments. Sportspeople and executives are continuously being coached to keep their mind razor focussed 'in the moment'.

What are the advantages derived from 'being in the present'?
CY: Living in the present makes you give your best at every moment. When your entire focus is directed on the present, your past and future recede to the back of your mind. You are not burdened with the memories of the past and the anticipations of the future. You feel complete, you enjoy more, you love more, you experience less stress, you have improved relations, you develop clarity of thought, you count your blessings more, you feel grateful, your physical and mental health are at their best; in short, you start living your life consciously, fully aware that each moment you breathe is a true gift.

Any quick tips for being in the present moment?
CY: Learn to slow down; learn to pause; learn to reflect; avoid haphazard multi-tasking; meditate; look to learn something from everyone; learn to see the lighter side of life; be a bit humorous; be adaptable and focus on value-based living and not result-based living. By practising being in the moment, you will be in a 'flow state', become a 'minimalist' and learn to appreciate everything that happens to you and develop an attitude of 'cheerful acceptance'. Another great way to remain in the Present Moment is to break

down large chunk of tasks into no more than 30-minute increments (made popular by the 'Pomodoro technique'). It helps you put a finite boundary around something which may seem overwhelming otherwise.

Shall we move on to our rapid-fire round, Yogi?
CY: Surely.

Rapid Fire Q&A on 'Past, Erase and Go'

How can I help employees to move from past-focus to present-orientation?
It all boils down to the conversations you have with them as a leader. Hence, you need to first learn and master the art of having conversations which are rooted in the present. Conversations should focus more on what can be changed and corrected now, instead of dwelling too much on what went wrong. Guilt-driven conversations should give way to positive, course-correction-related conversations. The same should be instilled in them so that they, in turn, have similar conversations with their team members as well. It will, still, drive positive results and performance. This kind of uniform approach, from top to bottom in an organisation, will contribute to increased performance levels and positive results. This could take any amount of time to settle down as a form of work culture, so, as the leader, you will need to be very patient as the employees tend to navigate away from these principles.

I can see some of my employees are bogged down by patterns from the past. How do I help them erase those (to the extent possible) and move forward?
If someone gets bogged down for too long, or grinds to a halt at some stage, it might be due to guilt over non-performance or poor self-esteem. Guilt is a common emotion that we all experience at some point or other in life, and if left unattended, it might even push one into depression. You need to make sure what kind of behavioural patterns they display; one of guilt or one of worthlessness (arising out of poor self-esteem). If it comes from a self-created image of

incompetence, you can boost their confidence level, by helping them locate the areas they are good at, and by pointing out where they have performed well. Guide them into the present and while doing so, also look for the emotions underneath the guilt. You would have to help them change their perspectives and move their focus from the past to the present. It might help to have periodical coaching conversations and counselling sessions with these people. Do whatever you think will help them develop or regain their self-esteem. You might want to consider having one or two professional counsellors (on roll or on call) who can help in parallel.

Teams, at times, carry debt of failures from the past. Can we transform their thinking to be more positive and future focussed?

It is natural, human and healthy to experience, recurrently, a range of feelings, including less pleasant ones like disappointment, dejection, apathy, or guilt. We need to go beyond the clichéd belief that positive thinking is the one and only way to set things right. Certainly not and one option is to turn 'positive self-talk' into 'interrogative self-talk'. Instead of positive statements (which of course work for a few), turn them into probing questions to activate deep thinking. For example, instead of making judgmental statements like 'I can do this' or 'I can't do this' ask yourself questions like 'Am I willing to do what it takes?' or 'How can I do this?' or 'When have I done this earlier?' This type of self-inquiry powers up problem-solving areas of the brain, helping you tap into your innate creativity. You will be able to greet negative thoughts or past failures or baggage with curiosity instead of fear. Look to focus on progress, not perfection. Be confident in telling yourself 'I am a work-in-progress and it's okay'. In short, learn reframing instead of just positive affirmations.

In addition, consider identifying internal coaches/champions—who can guide the teams towards the above outlook. Regular checkpoints to see how teams are faring will make a difference in the long run.

How can we ensure organisation learns from the failures of the past instead of getting bogged down by the baggage?

The wisdom of learning from failure is incontrovertible. Yet organisations that do it well are extraordinarily rare. Having said that, there will be very little to learn from failures if your approach is wrong. Leaders tend to look at failures as bad. Failure is not always bad. Sometimes it is inevitable and sometimes it can prove to be good. Perhaps, for reasons relating to Korporate Karma, you were being redirected to something better. One should not allow failures to lead to blame games ('procedures weren't followed' or the eternal self-serving 'The market just wasn't ready for our great new product' etc.). Leaders should be ready to jettison old cultural beliefs and stereotypical notions of success and be ready to embrace failure's lessons. It has a lot to do with Korporate DNA. You should accept and celebrate failures; and in extreme cases reward them.

Nature or Karma has found a way to stop you from going far in the wrong direction is another way of looking at failure. It might help you to refocus on a different path where better success may be waiting for you. In fact, a failure resulting after thoughtful experimentation that generates valuable information may actually be praiseworthy. If you were to analyse it, you'll realise failure could be a result of one or more reasons like deviance, inattention, poor capability, inadequate processes, inadequate resources, complex processes etc.

Use failures to build a lasting learning culture. Learn to create and reinforce a culture that counteracts the blame game and makes people feel both comfortable with and responsible for surfacing and learning from failures. Leaders should insist that their organisations develop a clear understanding of what happened; not of 'who did it', when things go wrong. This requires consistently reporting failures, small and large; systematically analysing them; and proactively searching for opportunities to experiment. Leaders could also learn to prototype before launching the final product or service. 'Fail fast, fail soon' models are gaining popularity world over and it is worth experimenting.

Are there effective strategies to coach my top-level leaders on structured ways they can transform their team members towards a positive outlook?
Strategies are decided by the outcomes you seek from them. Skills developed in the training room, in fact, transfer into the workplace as productive tools. It is truer with technical skills, such as the use of computer systems or customer service systems. It becomes very challenging with the so-called 'soft skills' such as coaching. For such transformational coaching, one would be best guided to take up 'evidence-based training or coaching' on a continuous basis. You should consider allowing for skills practice in the workplace (after every training/coaching session is over). Have internal peer coaching groups that meet periodically to take stock of situations. Whatever you do, focus on making it theoretically sound and practically grounded.

How can CEOs effectively learn from past experiences to shape the destiny of their organisation?
A CEO, typically, needs to be the driver of innovation and strategic thinking. He or she must make sure the company's expansion plans and initiatives align with the mission, vision and positioning. Along the way, the CEO monitors industry structure to ensure the company's offer remains relevant. While all this happens, they need to maintain their inner balance and harmony! There are a few things that they can surely learn from past experiences and dispense them away:

- It-won't-happen-again line of thinking.
- Refusing to learn from past experiences.
- Ignoring the usefulness of failures.
- Not tapping into external help (bouncing board).
- Micro-managing.
- Not being transparent, in short, not following credible values with people and process.

- Not being courageous enough to face the past in its entirety.

Alternately, they can build on the following to shape a better destiny:

- Learning to make balanced, democratic decisions.
- Being fully accountable for all actions and results thereof.
- Building further on confidence and self-belief.
- Continuing to be humble and grounded.
- Be inspiring and act as a positive role model to all.
- Further build on strategic thinking and execution capabilities.

How can a CEO bring in spiritual values into the multi-year planning process for a corporate?
It is not an additional planning input. It is one of the founding pillars on which the entire organisational edifice has to be built. The CEO and his team have to live and breathe consistently the values, planning being one of the activities that they dish out as part of their work.

As an individual, are there techniques available for me to alleviate my stresses at the end of each day and start the next day on a clean state?
For many of us, including CEOs, time is not the issue (which we think it is) but it is the energy that is demanded of us at every moment of our awakening state. The world is constantly, relentlessly asking for your mental energy. It is the 'energy sapping' which pushes people to the wall and make them feel toxic inside (and hence outside). That means you have to consciously decide where would you like to invest your energies. Minimum input and maximum output should be the way forward for CEOs. Here I am referring to 'energy', in whatever form one uses it.

One of the ways I would suggest you structure your day is that pre-lunch sessions be used for worrying about work and meetings, etc. Towards the evening, carve out time for work that is close to your heart and rejuvenates you, whatever it may be. Prioritise your day on this and don't compromise, come what may. At a lower level, at the end of the day, you can look at junk journaling (where you dump out everything that is bugging you as a way of emotional release), don't go onto social media post 6 p.m., stop checking into work every now and then (work will take care of itself), spend time on going within. The list can go on. My personal choice is 'rejuvenation through cleaning', a contemporary Yogic practice to detox your mind and soul of its daily baggage, complexities and impurities.

How to attract right employees, investors, vendors, partners and other stakeholders while getting rid of the negative and bureaucratic ones (who act like speed breakers for organisational growth)?

Talented and skilled people are always in demand. The more skill and talent they possess, the more likely they can leave you for another employer. Hence, you need to recruit right, train well and walk the extra mile in making them feel comfortable being with you. You can consider:

- Providing a positive working environment.
- You must continuously recognise, reinforce and reward your workforce.
- Stay involved and engaged with the workforce.
- Work towards consistently developing the potential of individuals.
- As part of wellness initiatives, allow them time to pray, meditate and do mental detox.
- Trust and respect them, all the time.
- Create and maintain a positive workforce community.

Employees who feel like they are part of the corporate family are the ones who stick around the longest. Hence the leader has to inculcate that level of trust and comfort them.

The following checklist or process might help you to achieve the above:

- Conduct exit interviews on the real reasons people leave your organisation.

- Ask employees who have been with your business longer than five years why they stay with you.
- Ask new employees what attracted them to your business.
- Evaluate which departments have poor retention rates and proactively take corrective actions.
- Create a retention plan for those key individuals that have the greatest impact on values, profitability and productivity.

Are there effective techniques to bring razor sharp focus in employees?
It all starts with your life and professional goals and how you prioritise your time. Given below is a checklist but you should tailor it to what works for you and your team.

- Remove distractions.
- Handle interruptions well.
- Keep clearing your mind of cobwebs.
- Break down large tasks into smaller, simpler chunks.
- Meditate and practice mental detox as and when you find time.
- Learn calming breathing techniques.
- Stay hydrated and stay nourished.
- Work within your energy.
- Rest well.
- Get comfortable with a routine.
- Start each morning with exercise or yoga.
- Have more Sattvic food.
- Set small daily goals.
- Focus on one thing at a time.
- Live in the moment.
- Every hour take a five-minute power break.

Looking Glass—Past, Erase and Go

Key Takeaways:

» At every juncture we have a choice to either react instantly or to pause, reflect and then respond.

- Immersing ourselves in the present moment is the key to undoing the past and recreating the future.
- To maintain your inner harmony or to be equanimous, one needs to let go of the focus on the results and instead focus on the efforts.
- Spiritual values are one of the key founding pillars on which the entire organisational edifice must be built.
- We cannot control what is in our COC but can control what is in our COI.

Action Points:

- Consider incorporating a programme around meditation or other techniques, which can help sharpen present moment focus.
- Engage professional counsellors for your critical employees who maybe prone to dwelling in the organisational past.
- Institute a governance mechanism and cadence, so failure can be analysed on a regular basis, and learnings extracted.
- Recognise and reward individuals who bring in enhanced present moment focus into their team's workings.
- Build a compelling story around your own failures and learnings as a leader—and share it with your leadership team.

8

The Metamorphosis of a CEO

na jayate mriyate va kadachin nayarh bhutva bhavita va na bhuyah)
ajo nityah) shashvato 'yam purano na hanyate hanyamane sharire||

This Self is neither born nor dies; nor ceases to exist again, having existed before; unborn, eternal, permanent and primeval; never destroyed when the body is destroyed.

||Gita Ch. 2–V. 20 ||

Abhimanyu—The Valiant

One of the most unique characters of the Mahabharata is Abhimanyu, the heroic son born to Arjuna and Subhadra. While Arjuna was revealing the secret of breaking into the virtually impenetrable army formation known as *Chakravyuha* to Subhadra, Abhimanyu absorbed the knowledge from inside his mother's womb. Before Arjuna could reveal the strategy of emerging out of the intricate formation, Subhadra went to sleep; Abhimanyu was left with the knowhow to enter the Chakravyuha but not to exit it. This eventually led to the tragic end of the young lad. Under the expert tutelage of Arjuna and Krishna, Abhimanyu was groomed into a courageous and dashing warrior par excellence.

At a critical juncture in the war, the Kaurava army formed the Chakravyuha and challenged the Pandavas. Arjuna and Krishna had the expertise to thwart the challenge, but the Kauravas adopted the wartime gambit of engaging them in a fierce duel far away, at a different front. Abhimanyu was chosen to lead, with a consensus that the other Pandava brothers would follow him into the formation and safeguard him. The strategic moves were in place and Abhimanyu, fearless and raring to go, rose to the occasion with absolute certitude about his pre-eminence, and successfully broke into the formidable cordon.

The Kauravas conspired to divert the rest of the troupe from following Abhimanyu into the formation, and engaged them in fights. Deep inside, Abhimanyu was left to face a direct confrontation with the stalwarts of the Kaurava army. The young lad of sixteen metamorphosed into an indefatigable warrior, not the least bewildered by the array of time-tested warriors before him, and fought with astuteness and valour. The fierce battle saw Abhimanyu slaughtering mighty heroes with relentless energy. When Duryodhana's son Lakshman was felled by Abhimanyu, Duryodhana was filled with rage and, throwing all the codes and ethics of battle to the wind, ordered his army to ruthlessly take on the raging boy. Abhimanyu, disarmed and overpowered, finally fell to the sinister moves of the enemy.

I am always fascinated by the heroism of this young kid, Yogi. Do you think there is a connection between Abhimanyu and the twenty-first-century CEO? Can you explain?

CY: Leadership is all about going through the process of metamorphosis on a perpetual basis. All the leaders who are on the path to continuous metamorphosis (it is a journey without a known destination, like all evolutionary processes) have one thing in common. They refuse to allow the conventional mode of thinking and practices, that once played a pivotal role in their past success (or failure), to become stumbling blocks on their way to the future. Abhimanyu knew what he was up to and who he was up against. He knew for certain, that the odds were heavily stacked against him. But Abhimanyu had his own set of values (perhaps that's where the word valour comes from?) and he was resolute not to let the Kauravas get away unchallenged; and he made the war of the Mahabharata take a decisive turn in favour of the Pandavas. A young warrior boy on one side, with no backup team and equipped only with his indomitable spirit, and the cream of the Kaurava clan on the other side; a David versus Goliath situation. Caught all alone, deep inside the Chakravyuha, with no knowledge of getting out of the labyrinth, the young man was aware of the vulnerable situation he was in and yet he chose the values of his legacy over his life. He went through the complete change management process and metamorphosed into an epitome of warriorship, all in a very short period of time.

Of course, he didn't pick up the mantle just like that; he grew up being prepared to face such contingencies in the battlefield. But what makes him stand out is his undeterred commitment to live by the standards of his father's reputation and deliver his best towards protecting his clan. He would have never even thought of withdrawing in fear; he took upon himself such a heavy assignment, notwithstanding his age. The beautiful budding life had to end abruptly; it was a heavy price the Pandavas had to pay and from then on there was no looking back for them. It looked like a mini battle within a battle and philosophically, that is how life is. What Abhimanyu demonstrated was classical 'situational leadership'. It doesn't come by virtue of position or experience, but through one's ability and presence of mind to stand up and be counted when it matters the most.

A CEO has several such chances in his lifetime to change, transform and metamorphose. The way Abhimanyu was closely watched by the Kauravas from across the battlefront, the same way a CEO too is watched. Whether he takes note of it and whether he makes it count, is a script up to him to write! Every organisation gets a CEO now and then who becomes the fulcrum around which all the major changes happen. He has to stand out as a true leader of men, not just by virtue of his post but by his thoughts and deeds.

What does it take to create such a leader? Moreover, what distinguishes a leader as one who has transformed or metamorphosed, in the first place?
CY: Simply put, it entails a process of self-cleaning, i.e., putting oneself through the process of cleaning and decluttering, inside out. To identify all the conditioned beliefs and dogmas, and the accumulated past, erase them all, and refurbish the mental space with a transparent and broader outlook and an expanded consciousness. This mental exercise is the root of transformation and you can yourself be aware of it as you start believing in rising up, declaring, and holding yourself answerable and accountable as the leader.

Leaders are authentic, being the cause (and not the effect) of everything; committed to something bigger than themselves; and as torchbearers of their proclaimed values, they have to exhibit remarkable integrity and a great deal of courage. This defining quality—a firm departure from what is known or established to what is unknown and cannot be predicted, needs loads of grit and boldness. The most important factor is, it entails pre-emptive, decisive action in the moments when it matters the most.

Such a transformation or metamorphosis—does it have any connection with AQ (adaptability quotient)?
CY: I just thought of this and there you are! It is said that true leadership gets expressed in one's ability to adapt to changes and the one who rejects or resists changes creates his own nemesis.

I want to draw a comparison with tiny microscopic aquatic creature called tardigrades, also known as water bears. Boil them. Crush them. They survive it all. They have gone through five mass extinctions and phoenix-like, they literally return from the ashes of their predecessors. The creature's adaptability to change in extreme conditions is the hallmark of its survival; when almost every other form of life vanished from earth, these grub-like, eight-legged, tiny creatures kept regenerating from decades-old dried out lifeless husk;

they can withstand near-zero pressure in outer space, the crushing depths of the Mariana Trench, and radiation levels a thousand times greater than the specified lethal levels for humans.

Can we learn a little from this life-form that has survived several billion years?
If only our hearts and minds are open, we can learn from all the other forms of living things that coexist with us on planet Earth.

What are the blocks that leaders might have to be wary of for being 'adaptive'?
CY: The biggest stumbling block is ego. We are infinitely small in the great scheme of things, yet many of us act as if we are in charge of this Universe. I recall the quote of Carl Sagan who said *'Who are we? We find that we live on an insignificant planet of a humdrum star lost in a galaxy tucked away in some forgotten corner of a universe in which there are far more galaxies than people'*. We are mere dust, totally inconspicuous in the vastness of the universe, yet we are not humble enough to learn and adapt to every situation that is presented to us as an opportunity to transform. Apart from ego as the biggest block, we have more smaller blocks in the form of lack of knowledge, reluctance to take on board others' viewpoints, a constricted view of the world, and may be many more. But the supreme 'block of all blocks' is our ego.

Where do you see the connection between spiritual values and metamorphosis?
CY: As a matter of fact, without the support of a spiritual intent and embedded spiritual values, the scope for great transformation or metamorphosis becomes narrower and narrower. The leader may or may not be aware of his spiritual inclination and values, but they contribute to a great extent for such transformation to take place. Transformation to a higher dimension needs a guiding force, kind of an 'Unseen Power', and a person's spiritual inclination and ingrained values become the subtle and unobtrusive guiding elements.

When your activities are guided by spiritual aspirations, they may not always yield the results you expect or wish for, but will yield results that you need to achieve. When you look at the lives of Prahlada or Abhimanyu, they both had a spiritually-inclined attitude towards life, and a clear understanding that there was a supreme force far beyond their comprehension. They had the capacity to do more than what they did, but they also believed that the Supreme Power had the final call. The missing dots are always connected in strange ways when you allow the Higher Power to work through you and for you.

A leader who is grounded, humble and in constant connection with the Supreme, will always be well guided from within. As I said before, the decisions he takes will automatically turn out to be the right ones and his moves will always be in the right direction, even if at times they may not be consistent and compatible with the ones expected of him by his organisation and his paymasters. The saying goes, 'Life is what happens to you while you are busy planning'.

A true Karma Yogi is the one who is aware that the best of efforts (lead indicators) are what he can do and the results (lag indicators) are purely consequences of his inputs. Get the input right and the output would, in all probability, turn out to be the right ones; may not always be what you wished for, but will always be what you needed!

Can you enumerate a list of qualities that an 'adaptive' leader should possess?

CY: A short list could be as follows:

- An elastic cognitive approach.
- Ability to use different and flexible thinking strategies and mental frameworks.
- Competence to question existing models, without fear or favour.
- High emotional flexibility.
- A sense of wonder and curiosity towards everything.

- Alertness and agility.
- Ability to distinguish between observation and inference, between fact and conjecture.
- An assertive nature in 'pushing the envelope'.
- Effective and comfortable handling of unexpected demands.
- Unwavering focus on the goal, but flexibility on the details.
- The power to turn anyone into a potential ally and strengthen your existing relationships.
- The natural capacity to be self-motivated and super-charged.
- Will power, compassion and determination.
- Readiness to face adversity, but remaining excited about solving the puzzles of life.
- A fresh, beginner's mind, not a jaded one.
- Compassion to listen to the heart and not the mind.
- Confidence to inspire trust in himself and others.
- The qualities of a rock and the vision of a prospective future instead of the short-term problems.
- A character of the highest order but also a chameleon-like ability to change colours to adapt.

Is transformation or metamorphosis a choice that a leader makes?
CY: Yes and no. When a leader is getting groomed, initially he may be a little orthodox and copybook type; once he faces real-time situations, he will gradually emerge out of the shadows of theoretical knowledge and settle down in an exclusive path carved out for himself, true to the adage '*Situations decide a man*'. Another way of looking at this is that sooner or later if the leader does not have a path himself, he or she will be forced to choose one by circumstances. It may be too late and the leader may not have enough time to plan and communicate the message of transformation effectively across his organisation. Hence it is good to be pre-emptive and proactive and be well prepared to set aside a unique path for himself.

Time for our rapid-fire round, Yogi.
CY: Sure. Let us move on.

Rapid fire Q&A on 'The CEO—Metamorphosis'

What are the top trends in transformation of the CEO's role in the digital age?
Organisations in all industries are wrestling with how to crack the code to win in the digital space. Typically, they focus their efforts on shifts in business strategy. They concentrate on enhancing marketing capability, creating new digital products and services, improving their social media efforts, and upgrading their IT expertise. But, as of now, it is clear that far less attention is paid to the important shift in leadership behavior that is necessary to foster a culture of innovation and experimentation. There is no magic formula for building a digital culture. It is always an ongoing process. The good news is, leaders don't have to be perfect in their efforts. They must have the courage to support experimentation and be ready to deal with missteps as learning opportunities. The big payoff is that leaders who take the time to build positive cultures and lead by example have a big competitive advantage to succeed in the race. In the digital era when things are moving at a fast pace, a leader who is always-ready will be able to respond to change in an optimal manner.

How can spiritual thinking complement disruptive thinking? How can it help in developing my innovative thought process?
Spirituality is a continuing process of disrupting your past and creating a new future, within yourself. This means that the 'viewing glasses' constantly keep changing. When the viewing glasses change, won't your views of the situations around you change correspondingly? What else can contribute to disruptive thinking better than a person's continuous transformation that keeps prompting him to refrain from looking at the present with

the viewing glasses of the past? In the same breath, it is sufficient to say that disruptive thinking, obviously, is interlaced with innovative thinking as well.

How can a CEO operate with an abundance mindset (rather than a scarcity mindset)?

Please bear in mind that 'abundance' is not about material wealth alone. When a simple rishi like Vasishtha could create for himself a cow called Nandini to give him whatever he needed, won't it be true of a person, at least at the thought level, to have an 'abundance mindset' automatically? The vast external universe is nothing but a manifestation of the internal universe (within each one of us). To understand the external universe and successfully tap into its perennial abundance of nature, at the thought level at least, you have to first understand your internal universe through simple techniques like meditation, introspection, contemplation and self-appraisal, and by being grateful, looking for opportunities in every situation, thinking big, embracing change proactively, working on expanding your consciousness etc. In short, one should develop the ability to tap into one's deepest inner self while allowing the universe to provide for your needs on an ongoing basis.

How have the expectations of employees from CEOs changed in the recent past? What are the expectations now, in the current scenario?

- Being consistent.
- Timely recognition and appreciation.
- Be a mentor, a role model and walk the talk.
- Appropriate and timely feedback.
- A well-designed work culture that fosters trust and respect.
- Allowing failures and experiments to happen.
- Putting people first.
- Being humble, grounded, honest and straightforward.
- Standing up for the team.
- Allowing merit-based organic growth within the organisation.

How to use the principles of karma to resurrect a failing business or a CEO?
Good and healthy seeds produce good crops; rotten and unhealthy seeds cannot be expected to produce good crops. The key is in the choice of the seed. While you still need to go through what you have sown (and hence what you may reap), it is absolutely left to the CEO (and his team) to make the right choices, based on spiritual values. 'What you sow, so shall you reap' has to be modified to 'What you choose to sow, you reap' (When 'choice' becomes conscious, you are careful about what you sow). Hence, keeping the spiritual principles and values in mind, the CEO has to go about making the choices and ensure the seed is chosen wisely. Making the right choice is 'cause'; worrying over the crop is 'effect'. The right karmic effects will flow out of the right karmic choices one makes. To make this happen, one needs to not only follow the right spiritual values, but also stay connected to a higher force.

Can spiritual values help a CEO in times of crisis and if so, how?
It is your character, which lets you respond to a given situation. Even in the current tough and abysmal situation that the world is going through (the COVID-19 pandemic crisis of 2020) you will see a plethora of responses from different countries, different organisations, different people, etc. How come each one is responding differently to a more or less similar situation? It depends purely upon their character, attitude, perceptional clarity, upbringing and personal values, which, I have to reiterate, are shaped by the presence or absence of spiritual values.

Even from the several sub-plots that you come across in the great epic, the Mahabharata, you will see that people don't view the same issue with the same lenses. Abhimanyu saw the situation based on his character attributes and his clarity of vision and purpose helped him to transform into a leader, taking complete charge of the critical situation. Look at the ignominious disrobing episode of Draupadi in the court of the Kauravas and how each one of the erudite scholars present in the court, including the one holding the highest authority, King Dhritarashtra, behaved; even though they all had to remain mute, each one was inwardly experiencing a different reaction. It is much the same for a CEO.

Both these events from the Mahabharata are extremely volatile, crisis situations of extraordinary magnitude. They are on the two extreme ends of a spectrum. One signified and glorified valour and the other demonstrated the callousness of outraging the modesty of a woman. The values or lack of values that each one held on to, influenced their choices, reactions and responses and that changed the story and how it unfolded. There is a lot that a CEO can learn, all the time, from the micro to macro happenings around him and he should keep checking his own thinking pattern to see where he stands vis-à-vis where he should be standing.

Does the heart play a role in the leadership of an effective CEO?

In some recent researches, it has been sufficiently proven that the human heart seems to have a brain of its own; not the standard way in which we understand brain as an intellectual faculty but as something that works exclusive to itself. You can find several references to this in scientific journals and the internet. People, and especially leaders, are classified as 'kind-hearted', 'stone-hearted', 'brave-hearted', etc. and, one thing's for sure, these attributes don't have any reference to one's brain!

All basic human qualities are always in connection with the heart, except the thinking part. After all, values create the qualities (and vice versa is also true) in us and those values and qualities together define what we are to the world. Hence, we can safely take it that the heart plays a major role in one's leadership journey. To give fair credit, women leaders score far better than their male counterparts, for a pretty simple reason. The heart is the seat of feelings and women, from time immemorial, are better at 'leadership through heart' than men. While strategy and numbers are 'head-based' stuff, predominant leadership qualities are 'heart-based'. The hallmark of a great CEO is a heart and head that are well-balanced.

How can a CEO strengthen relationships and garner respect from all levels of the organisation?

Let us look at the Mahabharata again. There were two pivotal figures that were consistently looked upon for their authentic inputs throughout; one was, of course, Lord Krishna and the other was Yudhishthira. If you dive deeper, you will find that both were *Sthitpragya* personified. Upholding Dharma (in current terminology, the Korporate DNA or values) was paramount for both of them, to the extent that even their sworn enemies, Kauravas, couldn't but admire them several times, even in the battlefield. If you have to derive an answer from this analogy, it could be their singular focus on their selfless concern for the well-being of others (altruism). Not easy to achieve but not outright impossible. Some of our great contemporary leaders often displayed this characteristic, like Mahatma Gandhi, Mother Teresa, and Nelson Mandela, to mention just a few.

What can the boards of companies do to effectively measure CEOs on aspects beyond hard financial results?

Boards are, in one sense, like guardian angels. They need to guard the CEOs and yet remain at a safe distance so as not to be intrusive. It is, in one sense, the board, through its actions and otherwise, which turns on the heat on CEOs. That makes or mars a CEO's thinking capacity to a great extent. Hence, the boards have a great role in shaping the character of a CEO, right from the time he/she is hired.

Many organisations, globally and in India, have taken a head start on this. You may call it the old TBL (triple bottom line) or the new TBL (incorporating spiritual values), but boards have started expecting their CEOs to go beyond just the numbers. They understand the innate value of a well-rounded CEO. It is yet to become accepted internationally as it is not all that easy for boards and organisations to look at the larger picture beyond just the financials, but the good news is, it is happening, slowly and steadily.

Boards must help CEOs look at the spiritual leadership aspect. It helps the CEOs to arrive at a balanced state by integrating power, love and leadership. The love here is like a tough love, which keeps the heart and mind in balance. It is said that a CEO directly impacts forty-five per cent or more of a company's performance (on all fronts). Boards should also help the CEO to build on the following:

- Have outstanding personal working norms.
- Have a social purpose.
- Help them measure and manage all cultural elements that drive performance.
- Help balance numbers and values.
- Make them look at building strong relationships inside the organisation.
- Build resilient teams to be ready ahead of any crisis.
- Mentor them to balance energy and time.
- Mould them to be authentic.
- Guard against hubris; rather guide them to be grounded and humble.
- Help them build a small group of trusted colleagues to provide discreet, unfiltered advice—including the kind that hasn't been asked for but is important to hear.

Looking Glass—The Metamorphosis of a CEO

Key Takeaways:

» The act of rising, declaring, and holding oneself accountable for being a leader is transformation.

» Ego can be one of the biggest stumbling blocks for a leader trying to be adaptive.

» A leader who is grounded, humble, and in constant connection with the Almighty, will always be well guided from within.

» Spirituality is a continuous process of disrupting your past and creating a new future, which applies to individual and corporate transformation as well.

- While strategy and numbers are 'head-based' stuff, predominant leadership qualities are 'heart-based'. The hallmark of a great CEO is a balanced heart and head.

Action Points:

- Introspect, as a group, about three instances from the past where the team could have responded to change in a better manner.
- Institute a 'Champions of Metamorphosis' programme to recognise and reward leaders who exemplified change.
- Identify the top three challenges for your organisation over the next few years where you will need to be proactive and ensure you have built a plan around it for effective execution.
- Identify instances in the past where you, as a leader, may have let ego come in the way of adaptability and how you should have responded in retrospect.
- Conduct a training programme around the concept of AQ (as a combination of EQ/SQ and IQ).

9

The New Terra Firma

gatir bharta prabhuh sakshi nivasah saranam suhrit
prabhavah pralayal sthanam nidhanam bijam avyayam| |

I am the Supreme Lord, the Sustainer, the Witnessing Consciousness, the Abode, the Refuge, and the Friend of all; I am their Origin, their Dissolution, their Ground, their Resting Place and their Imperishable Eternal Seed.

| | Gita Ch.9-V.18 | |

As this is going to be the culmination of the earlier eight chapters, I want to first present three fascinating stories from our epics, which I am sure, will add zest and flavour to our conversation. When Yogi began the ninth chapter with this introduction, I knew this was going to be a very lively and animated session on the topic 'The New Terra Firma'.

Story 1: Coward Turned Warrior

Uttara Kumara was the son of King Virata, who ruled the Matsya kingdom. The Pandavas spent a year of their exile living incognito in King Virata's palace. Uttara Kumara was a handsome lad, but he was a coward who spent all his time frolicking with women in the harem.

Duryodhana, suspicious that the Pandavas might be hiding in disguise at Matsya, stationed his army on the outskirts of the kingdom, preparing to launch an attack. King Virata was away with his army on a different mission and the news of Duryodhana's impending attack was conveyed to Prince Uttara Kumara, who with great aplomb, came forward to face them, bragging about his abilities to decimate the entire army. He took Brihannala, the eunuch, who was none other than Arjuna in disguise, as his charioteer and set out on his maiden battle.

The very sight of the vast legion of Duryodhana with the great warriors on the frontline sent shivers down Uttara's spine and the prince stood petrified. Unable to grapple with his mounting panic, he ordered Brihannala to turn back. Brihannala refused, citing a Kshatriya's dharma. The frightened prince dismounted from the chariot and took off on his heels. Brihannala chased and caught him and reminded the terror-struck prince of his noble lineage. He revealed his own identity as the great Arjuna and succeeded in motivating the young prince to retrace his steps. The emboldened prince was still terrified to face the great warriors, he preferred to drive the chariot while Arjuna fought single-handedly and made Duryodhana retreat with his men.

Subsequently, Uttara Kumara turned into a mighty warrior of great skill under the guidance of Arjuna and fought in the Mahabharata war on the side of the Pandavas. He met with a heroic death on the battlefield.

Can you explain the significance behind this story of Uttara Kumara?
CY: Before I go into the significance of the story, let me first explain the theme of this chapter, 'The New Terra Firma'. Terra firma is a Latin phrase meaning 'firm land'. Nervous flyers are generally overjoyed to put their feet back on 'terra firma' after a rough airplane flight.

In this continually changing melting pot of corporate life, reaching 'terra firma' is a dream for every CEO. Even if they reach 'terra firma', where things are settled, stable and more predictable, it is only a question of time before the earth below shakes again! Corporate and business life is akin to jumping into a pool that is muddy and murky and has varying depths. On top of all this, say, the pool does not conform to standard dimensions. Now, unsure of the contours of this pool, how will you jump in and come out safely, every time? I hope this analogy helps you understand how 'terra firma' assumes significance in the life or tenure of a CEO.

Let me get back to the story of Uttara Kumara. The story carries the message of how a coward, when asked to lead a high-priority mission, will fail miserably in the face of pressure. Similarly, a weak CEO will demoralise his entire team by his own incompetent and ineffectual approach.

In the case of Uttara Kumara, he was lucky to have the great warrior Arjuna himself pull him out of a pathetic situation. His initial reaction was to run away in fright; he needed someone like Arjuna to motivate him to turn back and confront the enemy. Still, the battlefield was terra incognita for the young man. However, he was able to transform himself from a shaky start to become one of the notable warriors in the Pandava clan.

Likewise, in a CEO's tenure too, there will be moments of crisis when he will be plagued by uncertainties and indecisiveness; to have a mentor who he can confide in and seek guidance from is essential. For Uttara Kumara, it was just a single battle to win, but it is altogether different in the case of a CEO who will have to face several battles, day in and day out. Technical knowledge, market knowledge etc., alone will not be sufficient and it becomes imperative that he draws energy and guidance from a larger-than-life source.

In the Bhagavad Gita, Lord Krishna says, 'Whenever action is performed by a great man, common men follow in his footsteps and whatever standards he sets by exemplary acts, all the world pursues.'

How does the concept of moving to 'terra firma' assume significance in current times?

CY: A 'terra firma' leader pursues his passion of being a catalyst in the professional and personal development of the people he interacts with. Let me throw some stats at you. The average lifespan of a company in the S&P 500 list was 67 years in the 1920s. Today, it's less than 15 years. Imagine the churn that is happening globally to have brought down the life of an organisation to just around 15 years. It is not that these organisations die or close down (some of them do) but they just stop growing and stagnate and eventually move out of the S&P 500 list. You can make the connection yourself. Unless a leader is continually trying to gauge the depth of an opaque pool, the chances are that he is going to have blood in his face—the equivalent of his organisation sinking.

What are the capabilities that a CEO should build on, in this process?

CY: First things first. Not just the CEO but the organisation itself (a broader responsibility falls on the board as well) needs to gear up. Isn't it a VUCA world, as it is called these days (VUCA is an acronym for volatility, uncertainty, complexity and ambiguity)? Companies have to adapt to new environments and situations faster than ever before, and the threat of macroeconomic turmoil and business model disruption is as high as it has ever been.

As a CEO, what can you do in the midst of these challenges? In difficult times, research has shown that the key is to instil trust, compassion, stability and hope in the workforce of the organisation (over and above the regular traits expected of a CEO). Let me elaborate:

1. Build trust: Good advice bears repeating. Trust building is a particularly old golden nugget that has withstood the test of time.
2. Show compassion: With trust serving as the bedrock of your relationship with your team, compassion is the humanising attribute for your leadership. When times are bad, your team knows to anticipate bad news.

3. Introduce stability: Many great CEOs opine that, 'Stability is something we don't often think about as a leadership quality—until it is absent'.
4. Positivity through hope: Hope will help set objectives, ignite the will, renew energy, foster creativity and innovation, focus on the organisation in turbulent times, and displace boredom and monotony. Hope provides the inspiration for people to keep doing the right thing. Hope defines what your team grows towards, in the way that plants reach for the sun.

Do you have a wish list for the CEO who is going through tough times?
CY: Foresight beats hindsight, every time. Let me give you a short checklist, if you wish to call it so:

- Control your fear.
- Remember that the mission is the topmost priority and that you are secondary.
- Rely on your preparation.
- Be tough but human.
- Encourage your people.
- Communicate effectively.
- Use your resources wisely; but use them you must.

How does a CEO handle his personal life during such times?
More than ever, it has become almost mandatory for the CEO to wear two hats, the business leader hat and the personal hat. You should demarcate the twin roles and set limits for each one, so that your concerns and responsibilities do not overlap and interfere with your doing full justice to the one that needs you most at that given moment. Of course, there will be dispiriting moments on either front that might spill onto the other, but you have to chalk out a personalised strategy to help you wade through and swap the roles in a discreet manner.

Your mood swings will permeate throughout the organisation, so you have to avoid a sullen disposition and keep your mood upbeat always. Your role as the CEO or the leader is to induce a productive environment, as free from stress as possible, even under difficult and unfavourable conditions. While you are in the process of handling certain critical situations, there may be temptations along the way, which you must take the utmost care to stave off. The kind of temptations one has to be wary of are:

- To spread a sense of urgency and panic. Instead of doing that, learn to break the news calmly, at the same time making the seriousness of the situation clear. Take a deep breath and carefully assess the situation so you can work with the team to set priorities. Your calm disposition will help you deal with the outer chaos in a much more balanced and effective manner. When a state of panic sets in, reactive leaders will ramp up the energy and stress in the atmosphere. True, that some problems may need to be solved *immediately*, but if the boss is frantic and emotional, everyone around will be too, and the efficiency and quality of work will diminish.
- To lay blame. Instead of doing that, help the team focus on moving forward. Ask, 'What do we need to do to recover quickly?' and then get the team to work together and make it happen. A team will be more successful by creating heroes who inspire others to step up.
- To let your emotions drive your response. Instead of falling for this, when your emotions flare, give yourself a moment to let your rational brain step in. Excuse yourself for a moment if you have to, or just take a few deep breaths. Find productive ways to channel the negative energy into positive results.
- To make assumptions. Instead of making assumptions, ask more questions that frame the big picture. Calm, value-neutral questions allow you and others to diagnose what is truly going on. Sometimes the team members know to pinpoint the cause of a breakdown, sometimes they don't, especially when there are a lot of moving parts in a lot of

departments. Often, a small issue that seems to be a choke point, happens to point out a symptom which in turn leads to a hidden systemic issue. Careful analysis with the team may bring to surface the core issues, which can lead to an exponential increase in efficiency.

- To publicly speak disparagingly of an imperfect employee. Instead of being loose cannon, if you really need to reprimand an employee, do so privately, in a journal or with someone unrelated to the office. When you're feeling calmer, approach the concerned employee directly, and in a polite but firm manner, share the truth about how they fell short of expectations.
- To withhold information. Instead of blocking information, give your people as much good information as the situation allows. Promise to keep them abreast and keep them focussed on the work they *can* do, rather than worrying about what they *can't*. That way, instead of tending to their fears and anxieties, you can lead them towards success.
- To softball criticism. You need to know how to package it well. Tackle the hard stuff first, directly and without hesitation. If they don't know they are creating a problem, they won't know they have to fix it. You can follow up with encouragement and praise to soften the blow without muddling the message.
- To draw comparisons between employees. This can be suicidal. Instead, evaluate each employee on his/her own strengths and weaknesses, using a clear rubric that is fair and equal for all. Base your comparisons on an ideal, not any one person, as your standard. Then take the time to work with each team member to invigorate them to perform at their personal best. Sure, you are busy, but making people believe they are the priority will motivate them to perform beyond their fears and concerns.

In this context, I would like quote a few lines from Swami Vivekananda's teachings: 'If you continuously hear bad words, think bad thoughts, and do bad actions, your mind will be full of bad impressions (samskaras); and they will influence your thought and work without your being conscious of it. In fact, these bad impressions are always working, and their result must be evil. The sum total of these impressions in you will create the strong motive or power for doing bad actions. You will be like a machine in the hands of your impressions, and they will force you to do evil. On the other hand, if you think good thoughts and do good work, the sum total of these impressions will be good; and they, in a similar manner, will force you to do good even in spite of yourself'.

Story 2: Mistaken Identity

Are not all of us potentially divine? This is a simple Advaitic story, which explains how one has to look into their inner self to realise the fundamental truth about one's real identity.

A flock of sheep saw a lioness on the verge of death, took pity on its little forlorn cub and decided to adopt it. The lion cub grew up among the sheep, behaving like them, bleating around like them, oblivious to its true identity.

One fine day, a lion chanced upon the lion-turned-sheep, sensed something was wrong and asked the little one who he thought he was. The lion-sheep looked frightened and replied he was a sheep and bleated to prove it. The other lion explained to the lion-sheep who he really was and to prove it, took the young fellow to a stream and made him look at his reflection in the waters. The little lion realised its folly, identified and accepted its true identity and happily joined its fellow lions.

That is an interesting short story, somewhat different from the other ones you normally share. Lion and sheep—do they have any symbolism in finding 'terra firma'?

CY: The Lion and Sheep story is a classical way to explain how and why many leaders and CEOs keep walking into the invisible trap—'the company that they keep (sheep in this case)'—all the time. It aptly illustrates how most of us, though originally designed to portray the powerful, magnificent image of the lion, are invariably born and brought up in the sheepfold of mortal weakness. We bleat with fear and death, instead of roaring with immortality and power and preying on wisdom and unlimited prosperity.

A few CEOs do break their 'sheep-hood' much ahead of others and have a different story to tell. The message behind this lion-sheep story should be followed as the basic guide for any CEO aiming to reach terra firma (and of course be ready again for the next round of seismic activities!). Situations will keep coming up to unsettle your equilibrium and you will have to rely upon your wisdom and not let go of the mighty spirit of a lion in action. Those who strive consistently, will not get bogged down by trepidation at the possibility of failures and defeats, and will learn to roar with the sanguine power of immortality.

The lion is an iconic symbol of unbridled courage, unfettered freedom and undaunted spirit; he never follows a crowd, he chooses his own direction, he goes to any length to defend his life, he never gives up his fight for what rightfully belongs to him; there he is, the unchallenged king of the jungle. If one wants to enjoy a lion's share in life, one has to have the attitude of a lion. You are endowed with a lion's heart and it is up to you to correlate it with a lion's attitude.

It all boils down to how confident you are about your innate strength and power. The highly efficient will be aware that regrets over lost opportunities will be more upsetting than failed attempts; they would rather go for bold action, even if they were unsure of outright success, instead of remaining inert. They know that no attempt is much more traumatic than failed attempts.

So, the bottom line is all about working to build the attitude of a lion?

CY: Yes. Your courage should reflect the image and attitude of a lion. Your attitude is the ultimate guide to your life; your thoughts, words and deeds, your reactions and responses, your rise and fall, your self-worth and self-confidence are all by-products of your attitude. You will realise that your attitude is improving and reaching a new high when you are no longer obsessed with what others think of you and start believing in yourself. Or when you move away from following the crowd on the beaten track and choose to walk the path less travelled. Or when you start looking at things in a positive and optimistic manner. All leaders were once followers and the paradigm shift in their attitude saw them reach the pinnacle of progress that changed the course of their lives. There is an African proverb: 'If there is no enemy within you, then no adversary on the outside can harm you!'

In the Bhagavad Gita, Lord Krishna, donning the role of Arjuna's charioteer, tries to dispel the fears and doubts Arjuna has on the battlefield by motivating him to pick up his arms and fight. The dialogue between Krishna and Arjuna gives us the impression that Krishna was trying to impose his will on Arjuna and force him to fight. We may think that Arjuna was trying to escape, but Krishna, through his intelligent arguments, was provoking him to fight. But that is wrong and the truth is, all the time Krishna was trying to liberate Arjuna, to lead him to his freedom. That is why Krishna kept telling Arjuna to identify his intrinsic nature, his self-nature, his intrinsic individuality, his primal being, his authentic face and *to be it*. The Lord kept telling Arjuna not to deviate from his authenticity, not to be in any way different from what he was intrinsically. The Lord was trying to expose Arjuna to Arjuna; unfold Arjuna to Arjuna. And after listening to the whole Bhagavad Gita recited by the Lord to Arjuna, had Arjuna still refused to fight and wanted to escape, Krishna would not have prevented him.

I am getting a hang of it, the 'terra firma'. Should we move on to the third story now, Yogi?

Story 3: Nala and Damayanti

Nala was the king of the Nishadha kingdom and was well-known for his skill with horses and his culinary expertise. He was invited for the Swayamvar (the royal function in which the princess of a kingdom would select her husband from among the suitors present) of Damayanti, princess of the Vidarbha kingdom. The princess chose Nala, a mortal, slighting the immortal gods who were also present. This incited the wrath of Kali Purush, an immortal celestial being, who vowed to ruin their lives.

Nala and Damayanti lived a happy life together for twelve years, had a son and daughter, before the evil designs of Kali shattered their lives. Possessed by the evil spirit, Nala became an addict of gambling, and a game of dice with his brother ended up in his losing all his wealth and kingdom. When asked to stake his beloved wife, he threw his royal robes in dejection, put on a piece of loincloth and walked out of his kingdom. Damayanti too discarded her royal clothes and wearing a single piece of cloth, followed him into the forest.

The evil influences kept playing havoc with their lives. Nala was bitten by a devil snake and was transformed into an ugly dwarf. His single piece of cloth was also snatched away by the wicked spirits and it seemed there was no end to his misfortune; and Nala, unable to see his wife's travails, deserted her when she was asleep, hoping she would be forced to go back to her father.

Both of them wandered aimlessly till they landed in different jobs in the royal households of neighbouring kingdoms. Damayanti was at last traced by her father, King Bhima and taken to his kingdom. With a view to unite his daughter with her beloved, the king arranged a second Swayamvar for her, in the hope that Nala would come to take back his wife. True to the king's expectations, Nala came and Damayanti selected him the second time as her husband.

At last, freed from the clutches of the evil spirits, Nala went back to his kingdom, played dice again with his brother, and reclaimed all that he lost, including the joy of a happy life with his wife and twin children.

This is indeed a fascinating story. The role of Damayanti seems to be equally powerful in this story.

CY: It depends on your perspective—how you choose to look at the whole thing. Let us first talk about a few varied perspectives and see if we can extract the maximum essence out of this story, to connect to our topic, 'terra firma'. Let us take Nala, the king, as a CEO here.

1. General perspective:

At the fundamental level, it is an engaging story about the enduring power of true love pitted against heavy odds. In keeping with the classical Indian tradition, Nala's story adopts the theological view that the destiny of each person is controlled by the merits and demerits not only of this life, but of the lives gone by. Life's events in the earthly existence do not occur at random or by accident; they are governed by the eternal principle of fate (Karma). One is nevertheless capable of rising above fate by dedicating oneself to one's duties and also to spiritual pursuits.

Grief and misfortune are the result of the negligence of one's Dharmic duty. In the case of Nala, waste of vital energy in material pleasures and dalliances with Damayanti, at the cost of royal and religious duties, are cited as causes for their sufferings. Reprieve came in the form of the divine serpent Karkotaka who led Nala to self-awareness, resulting in the subsequent reversal of fortune and the happy ending of the story. Faith in the ultimate power of divine grace has also been the core factor in the Indian belief system. The story of Nala and Damayanti reiterates the ancient belief in the role of fate in one's life and also advocates the equally efficacious faith in spirituality to transcend the miseries of life.

2. Woman as a powerful ally:

It was Damayanti's wisdom and shrewdness, on many occasions, that kept Nala in the game of life, and she excelled when she stage-managed a fake Swayamvar to get back the man of her life! In corporate life and even in quotidian life, patriarchy is the generally accepted norm of society and men tend to forget that it is the women who bring the balance in individual lives which men will never be able to achieve.

Right from the moment she spotted the original Nala (the devas appeared as Nalas too, during the swayamvar), and chose him as her husband, Damayanti was the one deftly steering their lifeboat through all the ebbs and flows. She finally guided her husband out of his abysmal state, back into experiencing the exuberance of life.

Behind the apparent veil of physical weakness that women seem to wear, there lies great strength that men will never be able to have or possess on their own. It can be called nature's way of balancing things. To reach 'terra firma' a CEO or a leader (assuming the reference is to a male) needs an element of diversity that only women can provide. They bring values (a few of which are listed below), that a man would find difficult to bring to the table. Each of the following salient points can easily be traced back to the Nala and Damayanti story.

- When and where to lean and when and where not to lean.
- Know one's limitations.
- Encourage transformation of people's attitudes and beliefs, and align people with meaning and purpose.
- Women put people ahead of themselves; they don't merely chase a bigger pay check, the corner office, a more senior title, or any form of status.
- Don't command; empathise. Twenty-first century leadership demands that leaders establish an emotional connection with their followers.

- Focus on elevating others by coaching, mentoring, and developing those in their influenceable circle.
- Women are humble. In the world of overconfident and narcissistic leaders, women bring humility (of course not all, but many).
- Look for what they can give; they always see a way to help on a project, as well as what they can offer you to succeed.

3. Belief systems, Karma and Power Politics (Nala being intimidated by Kali Purush because of envy):

In direct contrast to the characters of Nala and Damayanti is the portrayal of Kali, a powerful supernatural being as an evil character out to destroy the happiness of the couple. While looking at the intentions behind his actions, one can see jealousy, malevolence, hatred and cruelty embedded in them; Kali waited for twelve long years before the opportune moment arrived, and Nala, struck by the wicked influence of Kali, lost everything in the game of dice with his brother Pushkara.

People are always waiting for you to make mistakes. Corporate life, that too for a CEO, is not a walk in the park. There will be many who coveted that CEO's position but may end up continuing to work alongside as your teammates. Who knows where 'Kali' is lurking and in what form? All it needed for Nala's downfall was that one mistake he made after twelve years of a happy wedded life; your adversaries will wait for such an opportunity to strike the unnerving blow; it could be in any form; deceit, lack of cooperation, sabotage and many more.

I will share the following few profound statements from the Bhagavad Gita; Lord Krishna, during the course of His exhortation, tells Arjuna:

> *All those you think you have to kill are already dead. They are just awaiting death and at the most you can serve as a medium for hastening it. But if you think you will kill them, and then you will cease to be a medium, you will become a doer. And don't think you will be their saviour*

> *if you run away from the battlefield. That would be another illusion. You can neither kill them nor save them. You have only to play a role; it is nothing more than play-acting. Therefore go into it totally, and do your part unwaveringly. And you can be totally in anything only if you put aside your mind, drop your ego and cease looking at things from the angle of I or me and mine.*

How do you see the twenty-first-century CEO shaping up?
CY: 'It takes courage to grow up and become who you really are.'—E. E. Cummings

The twenty-first-century CEO has to be beyond the ordinary. A recent BCG report (Boston Consulting Group) suggests that the twenty-first-century CEO will be the one who balances three aspects: creating 'great company, great stock and great legacy'. A great company means strengthening of the company's competitive position and business economics. Great stock means delivering strong and sustainable total shareholder return and a great legacy means leaving a lasting positive imprint on the organisation. While it is reasonably easy to measure great company and great stock, as we can have objective measures to these two aspects, it is not easy to measure 'great legacy'.

> *You have a big canvas to make positive change and positively influence the lives of so many people. I hope they remember 'Performance with Purpose', the balance between the short and the long term, and making sure that large companies should deliver performance but also worry about societies and communities we serve.*
>
> —Indra Nooyi (Former CEO, PepsiCo)

As I see it, CEOs are more and more likely to become 'chief enabling officers' and not just remain 'chief executive officers'.

Will the 'Spiritual CEO' of the twenty-first century be known for certain values?
CY: They better be. **'V for Values; V for Vital Signs'**! As simple as that.

They are likely to display many or all of the following values:

- Happiness. Be able to express who they are.
- Less inner conflict. Have a balance between their outside actions and inside feelings and values.
- Better decision-making. By knowing themselves well, they are able to make better choices about everything, from small decisions like which dress to buy to big decisions like which partner to spend their life with.
- Display very good self-control. When you know yourself, you understand what motivates you to resist bad habits and develop good ones. You'll have the insight to know which values and goals activate your willpower.
- Resistance to social pressure. When you are grounded in your values and preferences, you are less likely to say 'yes' when you want to say 'no'.
- Tolerance and understanding of others. Your awareness of your own foibles and struggles can help you empathize with others.
- Vitality and pleasure. Being who you truly are helps you feel more alive and makes your experience of life richer, larger, and more exciting.
- Be well-grounded twenty-four seven; have a stable, grounded and humble disposition.

What would set them apart from the rest?

CY: Let us look at a short list:

- How they face hardships.
- How they act when they are upset.
- How they treat those who can do nothing for them.
- How they conduct themselves even when no one is watching them.
- How open they are to admitting mistakes and failures.
- How they treat people in need.
- How they respond to big failures.

- The choices that they repeatedly make in adverse situations.

How they answer the following questions, will also reveal a lot about them:

- What or who would you be if you knew you couldn't fail?
- What is your ninety-second personal elevator pitch?
- What are your core personal values?
- What makes you genuinely happy?
- If money were no object, how would you live your life differently?

If a CEO asks, WIFM (what is in it for me), how would you respond? My first response would be, 'Nothing and everything'. Nothing, if you look at it from an output (Lag Indicator) perspective, the game is already lost. You are likely to be yet another CEO who ran after numbers, profits and made your board happy, albeit in the short run. And everything, if you look at it from a transformation and metamorphosis perspective. You become a towering personality, someone your organisation, maybe even humanity, will remember and talk about for a long time. Your leadership methods might become case studies across your favourite 'B' schools.

Look at the life of several business leaders. They all had it made for them in their lives. Yet, they chose a far greater destiny of leaving a mark on the world canvas; of making a difference; of leaving an imprint which would inspire future leaders. If you are inspired by someone today, that someone probably did something extraordinary to stand out as an inspiration. The same way, won't future generations need personalities to look up to? There are people who watch the parade and there are those who make the parade and lead it from the front. Which one would you rather be?

There is a limit to the monetary benefits and corporate power that one can enjoy. Look at the turbulent time humankind faced during the COVID-19 crisis. You were at home and so were millions across the world. So what is the difference? A simple virus could put you under 'house arrest'. Yet, great leaders are needed to inspire generations to come and lead from the front after such crises tend to pass. Leaders have to learn to help their teams tide over such crises of great proportions. Be it defining and sticking to the core values, making the right decisions, ensuring frequent and timely communication, keeping responses humane—the list is long. The choice lies with everyone. It depends upon who would rise to the occasion—at an international, national or an organisational level. So, now you have to decide; what is in it for you or what would you want to make out of it for you? It is finally your call, you see.

Let me close this dialogue with one of my favourite quotations:

> *Our deepest fear is not that we are inadequate. Our deepest fear is that we are powerful beyond measure. It is our light, not our darkness, that most frightens us. Your playing small does not serve the world. There is nothing enlightened about shrinking so that other people won't feel insecure around you. We are all meant to shine as children do. It's not just in some of us; it is in everyone. And as we let our own lights shine, we unconsciously give other people permission to do the same. As we are liberated from our own fear, our presence automatically liberates others.*
> —Marianne Williamson (A spiritual activist, author and lecturer)

Rapid-fire Q&A on 'The New Terra Firma'

Where do we see corporates evolve to over the next few decades?

> We can't solve problems by using the same kind of thinking we used when we created them.
>
> —Albert Einstein.

Our lives reflect how we see the world. Practice viewing your life through different lenses and angles and this new whiff of thinking will bring in great ideas and lasting solutions. 'Leadership defines what the future should look like, aligns people with that vision, and inspires them to make it happen despite the obstacles,' says John P Kotter. The research work done by FW Taylor and Max Webber speaks volumes of the dire need for organisations to change their approach towards their people. According to Taylor and Webber, for more than a century, organisations have tried to control people through rigidity and fragmentation of work. Motivation was linked to their work output. Top managers had total control over planning and execution. But this approach wasn't working. If you want innovation and growth, you need to engage your people on a whole new level.

Top-down control is a thing of the past. Succeeding in today's environment requires a management style that inspires and is participatory. In 1999, the American Academy of Management launched a special interest group titled 'Managing Spirituality and Religion'. The findings mention Spiritual Intelligence as the secret for creativity, innovation, leadership and happiness. Spiritual Intelligence moved in and overtook the concept of IQ and EQ. Indeed, there was a growth in acceptance of the concept of spirituality in the organisations worldwide. Spirituality comes from the Latin word 'Spirits' or breath of life. Today, management and spiritual advisors unanimously agree that spirituality goes beyond religion. Spirituality is rather a feeling of being connected with one's complete self, others and the entire universe or is an 'awareness of being' or a 'force' that transcends the material aspect of life. Simply put: spirituality is a search for meaning in relation to the big existential questions.

From the above, it is quite clear that a paradigm shift has happened in the thinking of global leaders. It is yet to become a worldwide movement, but we are well and truly on our way. If you had a crystal ball to see into the future I think you would find organisations becoming more inclusive (both on the inside and outside) and look at operating more out of 'heart-based leadership' than 'IQ-based leadership'.

In the new world, how to gain a yogic like clarity and navigate uncertainty with ease?

Leaders who lead with their hearts in finding creative ways to solve challenges and heart-storming new approaches are those whose organisations will emerge on the other side of any uncertainty, more agile, more competitive and better off. To do this, you might need to check how you fare on this list:

- Choosing your attitude.
- Working within before working outside of yourself.
- Being reassuring.
- Rallying employees behind a shared sense of purpose.
- Acting inclusively: leading from the heart, not just the head.
- Practicing agility: building organisational resilience.

If history has taught us anything, it's that the worst of times can bring out the best in people—individually and collectively.

How to become purpose and impact driven (not popularity driven)?
To lead on purpose and create an impact driven organisation, one should possess six parameters—effort, enthusiasm, perseverance, knowledge, resources, and readiness to face obstacles; all these powered with God's grace.

How can a CEO and the organisation sharpen their relationships among partners, customers and employees in a world of increased globalisation?
The days of the dictatorial CEO, commanding imperiously from an exalted position are numbered, if not altogether gone. Think of yourself as a servant-leader, one who enables your teams to perform well and to collaborate with one another. Of course, you must set the direction, but after you've done that, you have to focus on motivating, inspiring, and encouraging. Whatever you do, don't meddle. It is crucial that you give others the responsibility and space to make the right decisions within an overall framework. As a CEO, you need to focus on the following to build an organisation that fosters healthy relationships among partners, customers and employees.

1. Positioning your company geographically.
2. Dealing effectively with rapidly changing conditions around the world.

3. Organising your company for the twenty-first century.
4. Developing a global culture.
5. Effectively leading a global company.

What is the role of spiritual leaders in guiding and influencing new age CEOs in the direction of compassionate capitalism?

Whatever be the benefits of spiritual leadership, capitalism (in some form or another) can't be taken away from corporate working and thinking. Hence, the term 'compassionate capitalism' becomes necessary. The money invested in business will have to give a ROI. Money by itself is no evil, whereas its deployment could be. Even to sustain 'spiritual leadership' you still need to pay in currency! Spiritual leaders will continue to play the role of Chanakyas and Krishnas, in some limited fashion. They are the ones who can safely be your conscience keepers and also help you to have candid conversations in times of ethical crisis. CEOs, periodically, need value, morality and ethics-based conversations, at least to clear their guilt. The spiritual leaders must share their insights with CEOs, which should transcend the financial perspectives alone and carry a 360 degree view. What could be the karmic creation of a decision, what could be the effects of a specific action, how to work on cause instead of effects, are just a few areas spiritual leaders can help and guide CEOs in. These can be mentoring conversations on an ongoing basis or specific interventions for a specific issue. Across the globe, even in communist countries, CEOs and top-level leaders are turning to spirituality for answers that they are unable to find through their management thinking alone.

In an era where loyalty to companies is vanishing, how can a Spiritual CEO drive better retention of key personnel?

Let us relook at what spirituality means in the workplace. A person's spirit is the vital principle or animating force traditionally believed to be the intangible, life-affirming force within all human beings. It is a state of intimate relationship with the inner self of higher values and morality, as well as recognition of the truth of the inner nature of others. Today, many individuals are looking forward to what spirituality can offer them at the workplace since this is where they spend the vast majority of their waking hours. The office is now the place where more and more people eat, exercise, date, drop their kids, and even nap. Many naturally look to their organisations as a communal centre because they lack the continuity and connection found in other settings. Moreover, recent polls have found that managers and leaders want a deeper sense of meaning and fulfilment on the job—even more than they want money and time off.

There is also evidence that workplace spirituality programmes not only lead to beneficial personal outcomes, such as increased job satisfaction, and commitment, but that they also deliver improved productivity and reduce absenteeism and turnover. Employees who work for organisations they consider to be spiritual are less fearful, more loyal, more ethical, and more committed. Moreover, there is mounting evidence that a more humane workplace is more productive, flexible and creative. Most important for organisational effectiveness, is the emerging research that workplace spirituality could be the ultimate competitive advantage.

Workplace spirituality is not about religion or conversion, or about accepting a specific belief system. Spirituality at work is about leaders and followers who understand themselves as spiritual beings, who have a calling that provides meaning and purpose for their lives. It is also about membership where people experience a sense of belonging, connectedness to one another and their workplace community. It begins with the acknowledgement that people have both an inner and an outer life and that the nourishment of the inner life can produce a more meaningful and productive outer life; this can have beneficial consequences for employee well-being, corporate responsibility and sustainability, as well as financial performance—in other words, the triple bottom line.

Let me share an interesting quote to conclude this matter:

> Religion I take to be concerned with faith in the claims of one faith tradition or another, an aspect of which is the acceptance of some form of heaven or nirvana. Connected with this are religious teachings or dogma, ritual prayer, and so on. Spirituality, I take to be concerned with those qualities of the human spirit—such as love and compassion, patience, tolerance, forgiveness, contentment, a sense of responsibility, a sense of harmony—which brings happiness to both self and others.
>
> —His Holiness the Dalai Lama, *Ancient Wisdom, Modern World: Ethics for the New Millennium*

How can CEOs rebuild their brand, from a picture of tough-minded businessmen to something more humane and compassionate?

We saw the answer to this in a different way in another section. Humans are often described as 'kind-hearted', 'warm-hearted', 'brave hearted', 'cold-hearted' etc. All these traits refer to the qualities of a person's heart. Likewise, there are also adjectives like 'cunning','crooked,'logical' etc. All these traits refer to the qualities of a person's mind. Toughness might come from your thinking whereas 'humanness' comes from a person's values that emanate from his heart. Like the jackfruit, which is rough outside but sweet and tasty inside, a sthitpragya of a CEO keeps an acceptable balance of mind and heart. The mind to help him and his organisation to produce the results, and the heart to keep the team and all stakeholders in peace and harmony. Hence, rebuilding a CEO's brand is to seek and find answers to becoming a sthitpragya.

Does prayer have a role to play in the reshaping of CEOs to develop more humility in their management style?

As you may have noticed, in several organisations and even in transit lounges of airports, there is a dedicated place for prayer (not worship, but prayer). Prayer is often used as the last resort, even by rationalists, at times of crisis and in some way to call out for support from a supreme force. On the other hand, prayer, as an act, is an acceptance of the presence of a larger-than-life figure or force in our lives. Prayer is not an act of weakness but it is an acceptance that not everything is solvable by one person or even by a group of people.

When you pray, obviously you accept the help that flows from somewhere in response to the prayer. Instinctively, we feel humbled. Prayer doesn't substitute efforts but is like a catalyst to move us towards the destination that much faster. Sometimes, the act of prayer helps the CEO to connect to a source within and helps in reshaping the destination, and for that matter the destiny, of the organisation itself. More than anything, prayer leads to the creation of a positive egregore (egregore is a concept representing a distinct non-physical entity that arises from a collective group of people) which rational minds cannot create.

Does acceptance have a role in the workings of a CEO—or is it seen as defeatism?

I would rephrase the question to say 'cheerful acceptance'. Cheer originally meant 'head' or 'face', with face in this instance representing the overall state of mind, or the mood. 'What cheer?' was an old greeting, meaning, 'what mood are you in?' or 'how do you do?' It is easy to imagine a gradual development into cheer specifying a positive mood, and cheerful meaning—as it does today—full of good cheer, i.e., in a good mood. Acceptance means the act of taking or receiving something offered (favourable reception, approval or favour). If you dive deeper into the practical significance of 'cheerful acceptance', it just shows that in some way, what happened was already set to happen, like karmic effect.

Once something has happened, does it make any sense to lament over what has already happened? Can it be changed? We discussed elsewhere that it is not time but one's energy, which needs to be managed during any situation. When you don't accept, but rebel or resist instead, you are fighting an 'effect' which has already taken place. Of course, you will still be within the limits of sanctity if you are to positively question and find out how to work towards changing further causes, on which you have control through the choices you can make. There is no such thing as grudging acceptance. You are either grudging or you are accepting. You can't be both at once.

Simply put, cheerful acceptance is a quantum leap in life.

Looking Glass—**The New Terra Firma.**

Key Takeaways:

- » A CEO needs to be strong; a weak CEO will demoralise the entire team.
- » A terra firma leader pursues his passion of being a catalyst in the professional and personal development of the people he interacts with.
- » Having a lion's attitude for a leader begins with how one thinks of themselves.
- » In the new era, CEOs are more likely to become chief enabling officers and not just remain chief executive officers.
- » Leadership defines what the future should look like, aligns people with that vision, and inspires them to make it happen despite the obstacles.

Action Points:

- » Develop a professional development programme for your top leaders.
- » For your target market and competition, define and elaborate on what VUCA (volatility, uncertainty, complexity and ambiguity) means.
- » Review past crises and introspect on how you could have demonstrated better leadership along dimensions of trust/compassion/stability and positivity.
- » Engage with your top leaders to brainstorm on how to

develop better organisation foresight to be better equipped for tough times.

» Develop a focussed programme to increase representation of women across the company from top leadership to individual teams.

10

The Last Chapter

I recall an anecdote from ancient Tamil literature involving poet Kamban, a legend in his time. Another poet in the kingdom of Chola, poet Ottakuthar, was equally eminent and of the same stature as Kamban. The story goes that both the poets entered into a competition to compose the great epic Ramayana in Tamil. At one stage, Ottakuthar was ahead of Kamban as he had already finished five of the total six cantos. Still, when the King asked for an update, Kamban, a master of words, lied that he was already working on Setu Bandhanam, which was in the sixth and last canto.

Upon hearing this, Ottakuthar got dejected and threw away his work. Feeling guilty, Kamban recovered the last two chapters of Ottakuthar's composition and added them to his work.

However, there is no such competition here. Mr Prakash is one of my mentors, and I am glad to contribute to this epic book.

I found the title of the book, *The Spiritual CEO,* unique and thought provoking. As I looked at the heading of the first chapter, 'Korporate Karma', I knew I was in for more interesting things. It set the tone for my review of the last chapter of the book.

It was fascinating to note that all the chapters of this book begin with a verse from the Bhagavad Gita and its interpretation, followed by interesting narratives from our epics or mythology. It is remarkable how it connects corporate matters with the spiritual essence contained in the introductory narratives. The book has been presented in dialogue format between a '*Corporate Yogi*' and a future leader, which is quite exciting. It provides a refreshing tone and tenor to a book on business matters. The oxymoron 'Corporate Yogi', coined by Mr Prakash, piques interest and kindles curiosity to find out more about how the term justifies itself.

As we move through the chapters of the book, you will see that the whole book revolves around the central and pivotal theme of how an ordinary Corporate CEO can transform and metamorphose into a Spiritual CEO. This process has been presented interestingly through a collection of stories and anecdotes from our epics and mythology. The book takes us on a fascinating journey through the rich heritage of our spiritual value system. Taking cues from our ancient teachings, it successfully delivers key action points and takeaways for the leadership-oriented business community to steer an organisation along the rightful course towards stability and success. It is noteworthy how the narrative keeps going back and forth through the chapters to integrate the practical application of the various insights and action points mentioned in the book.

I think it is best to discuss the book chapter-wise and elaborate on the topics discussed therein. This is to do justice to the structured approach, meticulously planned and adopted by the author.

Chapter 1 (Korporate Karma) dwells on the influence of Korporate Karma on organisations and their leaders. This is achieved through hypothetical comparisons of how Karma casts its powerful influence on the lives of the various puranic and mythological characters. We can get an idea of how Korporate Karma gets formulated as a fundamental factor while conducting business and how its effects can make or mar the future of an organisation or a leader. Perhaps that is why I believe Mr Prakash starts the book with 'Korporate Karma' as the first chapter, to give it the priority it deserves.

Korporate Karma is defined in the most precise and thought provoking way as: 'What gets passed down to you from your predecessor in this pivotal role of a CEO is not mere knowledge about finance, products, customers, etc. You will also be inheriting a huge balance of the Korporate Karma set to play a crucial role in steering the course of the ship during your tenure'. It is so true that we often get stuck and concentrate on our inherited issues and seek to solve only that. This mindset is so powerful that most of the time, it reduces our actions to being mere reactions to what is happening around us, instead of producing concrete and viable results.

Korporate Karma has two sides: what you inherit from your predecessors and what your successors inherit from you. When a new CEO takes charge of the organisation, the first thing on his mind should be the kind of inheritance and legacy he should leave behind at the end of his tenure. This awareness is emphasised since it is a crucial aspect to be considered by an organisation and its CEO. To defend a business and guide the lead indicators, there can be no better way than to keep a constant check on the status of the Korporate Karma that gets accrued by the organisation or the CEO.

Chapter 2 (Spiritual Alchemy—The Quintessential Formula) talks in detail about the furtherance of a CEO's role. The author elaborates on the need for a CEO or leader to identify his enormous potential and channelise it to build a position for himself and the organisation.

He stresses the need for constant and unflinching efforts to become better versions of themselves and achieve effective and dynamic leadership qualities.

The two main avatars discussed in this book, Lord Rama and Lord Krishna, stand as ideal examples in this regard. Lord Rama was the sole and independent authority among his clan, while Krishna exercised his authority, wherever necessary, and influenced others' behaviour in distinct ways. It is also important to note that Rama's incarnation preceded Krishna's, and the former showed everyone how to be a righteous leader in every aspect. The latter taught everyone how to transform into better personalities. The very phrase, 'It is for mere mortals, Arjuna!' holds for a leader or a CEO. A CEO should stand tall and think and act big; 'The limitations may apply for a normal team member and not for a leader'.

The book emphatically states that transformation into higher states has to be given priority over the deliverance of results. 'Going Concern' as a concept is not for legality only but for every action of the CEO.

Hence, 'What to achieve' is just a starting point; 'why and how' become continuous efforts towards transformation. As a practitioner and trainer, Mr Prakash has articulated the importance of the movement to higher and broader levels of thinking, in tune with the prescribed values of spirituality.

Spiritual Alchemy is aptly defined as 'the process of taking something ordinary and turning it into something extraordinary'.

Chapter 3 (Cause and Effect—Where is Your Focus?) recommends striking the perfect balance between the materialistic and the value-based approaches to leadership as an essential requirement for business success. It is not just financials anymore; it is much more than that. The Cause and Effect theory is the basis for the buildup of Korporate Karma. Business leaders need to be mindful of this while the strategic planning for a business's future development is being discussed.

By raising the question, 'Where is your focus?', leaders and CEOs are reminded of the truth that they are vulnerable to the Cause and Effect theory and they have to make themselves accountable for the 'what, why and how'. Mr Prakash makes a valid point that the Cause and Effect theory applies to all, irrespective of their position and status.

Chapter 4 (It Is Not Just the Financials Anymore—Corporate TBL and Spiritual TBL) explains how to acquire coveted leadership qualities. An efficient leader has to seek and identify the potential for dynamism and broad-based values within himself and channelise them to contribute to his team's overall performance and the organisation's success. Merely following the externally acquired skills and theoretical/practical knowledge may not take him to new heights. He must focus on his self-development and the development of his team. At some stage, he could find that his own development may cast its positive vibes on his team members. A multi-dimensional approach by the leaders, emphasising progressive values and team spirit, is an essential requirement for the organisation's growth.

'Many corporate organisations demonstrate a short-minded approach in the quest of only one thing, the financials, while a broader perspective is what is called for'.

Chapter 5 (The Korporate DNA—A Place for Shared Traditions, Values and Beliefs) explains that the DNA of an organisation is the combined value system developed and followed by the leader and his team in a spirit of integration and coordination. 'A Spiritual CEO would be more inclined towards building a team of winners, by infusing high values and an element of cultural identity, which would eventually translate into and reflect as positive responses in everyday activities'.

The high values should not be merely talked about or exhibited, but should get reflected in the everyday activities of the entire workforce. The rich legacy and traditions of the organisation should be preserved and passed on to the new incumbents. A lot is conveyed through this powerful insight, 'A king does not abide within his tent while his men bleed and die upon the field. A king does not dine while his men go hungry…'

It can easily be concluded that being a CEO is a huge responsibility and not an inherited property to enjoy. He has to keep on refining himself and empowering his men to move up the ladder of success. 'Leaders have to become walking ambassadors of

Korporate DNA and the proclaimed value statements' is the key takeaway here.

Chapter 6 (Who is a Spiritual CEO? The Conundrum of Body, Mind and Soul Being in Balance) discusses that as human beings, we know we are all under the direct control of the body, mind and senses. Yet, we tend to forget the soul, which is very subtle and has to be nourished through only subtle spiritual practices. Mr Prakash himself has been into the spiritual practice of meditation for over three decades, and there's none better than him to provide such valuable spiritual inputs as to be found in this chapter.

The central point of the discussion, in this chapter, is how leaders have to take care of themselves and their organisation. A balance should be struck wherein one aspect of life should not get compromised for the sake of the other. The secret to this lies in maintaining a healthy physique and an equally healthy mind.

The chapter provides valuable information on how food habits influence a person's character traits. A healthy mind and behavioural tendencies can be developed by bringing spiritual values and ethics into one's way of living.

Chapter 7 (Past, Erase and Go) begins with a narrative about how Sage Viswamithra, a King of his time, makes himself deserving of the most prestigious and highest title of Brahmarishi. Each step he contemplates requires him to erase his past through the difficult path of strenuous penance towards self-realisation.

Sage Vishwamitra's determination to reach his goal, surmounting all the hurdles and impediments in the path, is an example worth emulating by goal-oriented leaders or CEOs.

The present moment is the only available time to act, and leaders can achieve their goals faster if they focus on the present moment. They should avoid brooding over past failures, stop anticipating troubles in the future and proceed towards their goals undeterred by the interruptions in the process.

It is a wrongly held belief that time is under our control and we can manipulate it to our convenience. The truth is, we are bound by time and the more we allow ourselves to understand it and its unpredictable nature, the better it is for us, as we can then make use of the present moment and move towards our goals.

God does not deliver human beings as finished products; they are in the WIP (Work in Progress) mode. They have to keep on striving to evolve and transform into better versions of themselves. Such thinking will bring humility and allow one to integrate and work in harmony with others. Leaders should avoid pride and vanity over their successes and achievements, which distances and alienates them from the other members of the organisation.

Chapter 8 (The Metamorphosis of a CEO) brings out the complete picture of how a Spiritual CEO should be. It proceeds to explain how a CEO should metamorphose into the highest version of himself. In every situation, despite being possessed with all the knowledge and perfect alignment of mind, body and soul, a CEO will find particular challenges too much to handle.

A warrior cannot turn his back on the battlefield, even during a threatening and critical situation. To understand this, there is no better example than Abhimanyu. He knew he did not possess the knowledge to come out of the enemy's complicated army formation, yet he never thought of withdrawing. Instead, he plunged into the task of confronting the enemy and, to safeguard his own men, sacrificed himself. This kind of selflessness is the key to the success of a CEO.

Standing up to situations that call for sacrifices will eventually take the CEO to the greatest heights.

This statement provides great insight for a leader, 'When a leader is getting groomed, initially he may be a little orthodox and copybook-type; once he faces real-time situations, he will gradually emerge out of the shadows of theoretical knowledge and settle down in an exclusive path carved out for himself, true to the adage, 'Situations decide a man'. Another way of looking at this is that, sooner or later, if the leader does not have a path himself, he will be forced to have it by circumstances'.

There is a verse in Tamil from Thirukural, which translates to 'Despite having a great army, it will be of no use, unless it is guided by a great general'.

The chapter talks about metamorphosis, not as something that happens on the physical level, which the term literally stands for, but takes us deeper into the process and gives a vivid description of how the transformation can happen at the core levels of a person.

Chapter 9 (The New Terra Firma) is the culmination of all the previous chapters. The leader or CEO who is capable of understanding the nuances of combining spiritual values into his self-development and the working of his organisation, will be the one who can finally qualify as a 'Spiritual CEO'.

It is a possibility that some might give up midway and be ready to take flight like Prince Uttara Kumara when he had to face a formidable army in battle. But we can see how the same cowardly prince gets his training under the gallant Arjuna and eventually proves himself as a warrior par excellence in subsequent battles.

A CEO is also expected to continuously undergo the transformation process until he reaches the pinnacle of his career. The chapter explains the leader's role during critical situations in his organisation and how his confidence in tackling the crisis period, with composure, will go a long way in keeping the spirits of his team up about the future of their business house. The team always follows the leader. Hence, it becomes important for the leader to instil hope and confidence in his team members and motivate them to rise, even during critical situations.

Failure could lead to frustration and demoralise and demotivate the entire team, including the leader. The onus is on the leader to tide over the crisis with equanimity and cooperation from his teammates. A Spiritual CEO, supported and energised by spiritual values, will be better equipped to handle such challenging situations with levelheadedness.

It is notable that the author does not miss the practicality of the situation when he explains how the CEO, despite problems at work, should take care that it doesn't spoil the peace and harmony of his personal life.

Before I conclude, let me share a few more words about the book and my longtime association with the author, Mr Prakash.

I'd like to quote an English translation of a verse from Thirukural, which relates to the duty of a leader/CEO.

> *A King is one who treasures gains, stores up, defends his kingdom and works on its expansion.*

This verse from Thirukural has stood the test of time for over 2000 years, and though originally meant for kings, holds true for CEOs in the modern day. It does not talk about the past but about the present and the future. The same message is conveyed through the different chapters of this book.

Mr Prakash has had a great influence on my thought process. He has mentored me on many occasions, and we have had discussions on many subjects related to the corporate world. We often discussed the need for CEOs to be guided by spiritual values instead of allowing themselves to be influenced by the temptations (spirits and alcohol) of corporate parties and gatherings, where the focus for building consensus is on entertainment value.

The good thing is, a change for the better is happening, especially in the context of the Covid-19 pandemic and lockdown. Spiritual thoughts and values are taking precedence over other mundane activities, and its positive effects are already surfacing in the form of better results achieved by the IT sectors

The book builds various characteristics of leadership in a phased and gradual manner. Mr Prakash emphasises the importance of creating and maintaining a coordinated and harmonious work environment and culture, for both employees and CEOs. Stress is laid on CEOs developing a good rapport with team members; customers, vendors, employees, and regulators contribute to a collective spirit of adopting certain intrinsic ethical values for the organisation and its CEO. Such an organisation will prove to be much more successful. Building a balanced approach is elaborated well in detail and with much clarity by the author, he himself being a person of vast experience in the business world.

The book is '***A must-read for anyone aspiring to transform from an ordinary leader into a Spiritual CEO.***'

With sincere gratitude, I express my thanks to Mr Prakash for bringing out this wonderful book.

Kumar Rajagopalan, vice president and country head, DISYS India Pvt Ltd